T0072913

THE FOOD DEHYDRATING BIBLE

Grow it. Dry it. Enjoy it!

THE FOOD DEHYDRATING BIBLE

Grow it. Dry it. Enjoy it!

BRETT L. MARKHAM

Skyhorse Publishing

Copyright © 2014 by Brett Markham

All rights reserved. No part of this book may be reproduced in any manner without the express written consent of the publisher, except in the case of brief excerpts in critical reviews or articles. All inquiries should be addressed to Skyhorse Publishing, 307 West 36th Street, 11th Floor, New York, NY 10018.

Skyhorse Publishing books may be purchased in bulk at special discounts for sales promotion, corporate gifts, fund-raising, or educational purposes. Special editions can also be created to specifications. For details, contact the Special Sales Department, Skyhorse Publishing, 307 West 36th Street, 11th Floor, New York, NY 10018 or info@skyhorsepublishing.com.

Skyhorse® and Skyhorse Publishing® are registered trademarks of Skyhorse Publishing, Inc.®, a Delaware corporation.

Visit our website at www.skyhorsepublishing.com.

10 9 8 7 6 5

Library of Congress Cataloging-in-Publication Data is available on file.

Cover design by Kisscut Design

Print ISBN: 978-1-62914-181-7
E-book ISBN: 978-1-62914-286-9

Printed in China

Contents

Introduction.. ix

Chapter 1: Principles of Dehydrating................................. 1

Chapter 2: Dehydrating Fruits... 13

Chapter 3: Dehydrating Vegetables................................. 31

Chapter 4: Dehydrating Meat and Fish............................. 43

Chapter 5: Dehydrating Breads....................................... 57

Chapter 6: Dehydrating Herbs and Spices....................... 65

Chapter 7: Making "Instant" Foods.................................. 71

Chapter 8: Recipes... 81

Chapter 9: Build Your Own Dehydrator............................ 95

Notes 121

Recipe Journal.. 133

This book is dedicated to my father who imparted a million skills to me that I never thought I'd need, but that have added immeasurably to my life, and to everyone who has to figure out how to make ends meet with far too few dollars.

Introduction

In the mid-1990s I joined the ranks of what are known as "the working poor." I lived alone in a small studio apartment. Between the costs of rent, car insurance, child support, gas to get back and forth to work, and other necessities, my weekly food budget was only thirty dollars. The simplest things, such as a flat tire, would set me back so that I couldn't afford to pay my electric bill on time and all the food in my refrigerator went bad.

I was very cognizant of the need for a balanced diet including plenty of vegetables and fruits. But buying them fresh was often cost-prohibitive, and most canned vegetables from the supermarket are less nutritious than fresh or frozen ones.

During that time, I grew my first gardens since moving to New England from Virginia. A studio apartment affords no ability to garden, and there were no community gardens nearby. So I made use of a plot of ground that I tilled at the edge of some high-voltage lines, and grew some vegetables that way.

The local grocery store would take fruits and vegetables that were past their peak and couldn't be sold at full price, mark them down, and put them on a carousel. This allowed me to buy a variety of vegetables and fruits for far less than retail, though I'd have to remove rotted spots and use them almost immediately. Unfortunately, the supply of vegetables that way was intermittent at best. The store would do the same thing with meats, marking them down the day before they were to be discarded.

This is when I got into dehydrating. I invested $50 in a dehydrator from a large chain store, and used it to preserve food when I could get it, so I'd have it for later, whether my electric bill was paid or not.

At that time, I did a lot of Thermos™ cookery. Instead of buying bread or boxed cereal, I'd buy hard red winter wheat berries, rolled oats, or plain rice cheaply, and cook them overnight in the thermos. When I started dehydrating food, my thermos cooking really took off because I could then add dried apples or strawberries to my concoctions. Even more importantly, I could make hearty soups and stews from jerky and dried vegetables. When summer came, my small plot under the power lines yielded produce that I could dehydrate to keep me through the upcoming winter.

Between the hidden garden, buying nearly-expired food at the supermarket, and using plain grains instead of processed foods, I was able to thrive, rather than merely survive, on my meager food budget.

Eventually, things started to look better for me economically. At this point, I don't need to dehydrate, grow a garden, or pinch pennies the way I had to back then. But I do it anyway.

For those who have read my other books, you know that I use a method I call "Mini Farming" to provide 80% of my food. Before I adopted the Paleo™ diet, I made my own breads, cheeses, and beer. I continue to make my own wine and vinegar. I can reliably pay my electric bill these days, so I freeze a lot of food for preservation, and because I have more space, I do a lot of canning as well. But I still do a ton of dehydrating.

Even though it may not be necessary, by growing and preserving food at home, your family saves a lot of money. More importantly, it turns the home from being little more than an expensive hotel that costs money into a center of production that pays for itself. Even better, as I document more fully in *The Mini Farming Guide to Vegetable Gardening*, food you grow yourself can be dramatically more healthy and rich in life-sustaining nutrients than food you buy. In addition, the movement and exercise involved in gardening is healthful, and the time spent interacting with nature is therapeutic.

Dehydrating is the oldest means of food preservation, and it is one of the most convenient. The food will keep even if you've lost electricity due to a storm. It also weighs a lot less, and takes up less space than any other method. I have dehydrators sized for small jobs, and a large dehydrator for large harvests. These allow me to save food either in batches or "off the cuff." And the dehydrated food supplies add up. I have dehydrated beef, fish, parsnips, carrots, celery, tomatoes, peppers, beets, and herbs on hand, among other things. Using these ingredients, I can do everything from thicken spaghetti sauce for canning through making a complete beef stew.

The greatest recommendation I have for dehydrated foods is that they are convenient, and lend themselves to making convenience foods ranging from packaged salad dressing mixes through mushroom soup. They are likewise tasty!

I've done a lot of dehydrating over the past twenty years. Taken as a whole, dehydrating is very simple so it doesn't need a weighty tome to reveal its secrets. What I have done in this book is to describe the underlying principles and practices of dehydrating in such a way as to remove any mysteries or apprehensions, and also describe the practical use of dehydrated foods in a way that makes them enticing. Dehydrated foods have a place in your cooking and diet, and that place can be delicious!

Chapter 1
Principles of Dehydrating

All forms of food preservation work by slowing or stopping the processes that cause food to spoil, degrade or rot. Wine preserves juice by replacing sugar with alcohol. Brined pickles preserve cucumbers by converting sugar to lactic acid. Freezing food preserves it by slowing enzymatic processes and making it too cold for spoilage organisms to reproduce. Canning preserves foods by killing spoilage organisms, deactivating enzymes and excluding oxygen. Dehydrating works by removing the water necessary for enzymes to work and spoilage organisms to live.

Why Foods Rot

Everything produced in nature returns to nature. The leaves that fall from trees ultimately become the soil from which trees draw sustenance to make new leaves. Although sometimes food takes a more circuitous route to its ultimate destination, this is the fate of all things. Nature assures this outcome in the very mechanisms of cells.

When a cell is cut off from its supplies of food and oxygen, as happens to the cells of a steak when a steer is killed, the enzymatic processes in the cell don't simply stop. In fact, those processes can continue for many days depending upon the conditions under which it is stored. However, the processes are not those that normally take place while the animal is alive. During life, metabolic waste products such as lactic acid and carbon dioxide are removed and replaced with fresh glucose and oxygen. This allows the cell to operate effectively. But when waste products are no longer removed and new supplies are no longer delivered, the proteins and enzymes within the cell take on a different character and purpose. Specifically, proteins are created that tear down tough tissues and collagen so that the meat can be more easily digested by microorganisms such as bacteria and macroorganisms such as fly larvae.

While the process of aging meat is sometimes thought of as being a form of rotting, it actually isn't rotting because it doesn't utilize spoilage organisms. Rather, aging takes place at temperatures that discourage rapid bacterial growth while still allowing the after-life enzymatic processes of the cells to tenderize meat so it is more flavorful. Of course, if the temperature were a bit too high or it was kept unfrozen for too long, the tenderized meat would be a prime meal for microorganisms that would induce rot in short order.

The same thing occurs in fruits and vegetables. For example, when making brined pickles, the blossom end of the cucumber is sliced off so that the enzymes don't spread throughout the cucumber and soften it.

So the first cause of food spoilage is enzymatic. Enzymes within the cells of a food product will break it down, soften it, and make it ready for consumption by microorganisms such as fungi and macroorganisms such as fly larvae. These enzymes don't actually spoil the food, but they make the food susceptible to spoilage organisms and alter its character.

Another cause of food spoilage is microorganisms. With the exception of pathogenic diseases, occurring while something is alive and exchanging sustenance, microorganisms seldom have much of an effect. An apple on a tree seldom spoils, spinach leaves on a plant don't spoil, and chickens walking around the yard are unaffected by bacteria. It is only after the cells of the plants or animals are no longer receiving new sustenance and their waste products are no longer removed that they become vulnerable to spoilage.

Of course, we don't usually eat apples right off the tree or pick up a chicken out of the yard and eat it whole on the spot complete with feathers. Instead, these are processed and shipped or harvested and stored. And it is the time after harvest or processing that creates the window of vulnerability for microorganisms.

Microorganisms that are utterly harmless to living things get busy in a hurry on processed and harvested food. As they consume the food, they grow their own populations and return the nutrients in the food to the earth to repeat the cycle. When this happens in your compost pile, that's a good thing. When it happens on your kitchen counter to organic peaches that cost $5/lb., the event is less amusing.

Microorganisms are no different from any other living thing in that they require certain conditions in order to thrive. Some microorganisms require oxygen, and some can't grow while oxygen is present. Some microorganisms grow best at room temperature and others grow better at slightly higher or lower temperatures. Every microorganism also has certain preferred ranges of food. This means that they will grow in some foods, but not in others.

These two factors—cellular enzymes and microorganisms—are the key factors in food spoilage. Other factors can contribute to these processes and may even be prerequisites, but enzymes and microorganisms are the key.

Sunlight and other sources of bright light also play a role in spoilage because the ultraviolet rays can discolor or damage food. Another source of damage is oxidation. You've seen this with a cut potato or apple changing color. Though the changes made by sunlight and oxidation aren't as serious as those made by enzymes and microorganisms, preventing them is important for making an appealing product.

How Dehydration Keeps Food From Spoiling

Water is necessary for life and all of the processes of life. No water means no life. Although this may only be a problem if you've decided to hike through the Sahara desert, it is also useful knowledge for preserving food.

Water is the carrier within cells that allows enzymes to function. If the water is removed from the cell, then the enzymes are stopped in their tracks. Most enzymes have a particular temperature range at which they work. Freezing preserves food by holding enzymes below their operational temperature range. Canning preserves food by raising the temperature so high that the enzymes are denatured so they are broken down and can therefore do nothing. Dehydration works by removing the water that enzymes need in order to function. It is important to understand that the enzymes can be (and often are) still present in dehydrated foods, but are simply inactive due to a lack of water. Once water is added, enzymatic action and consequent degradation returns.

Freezing controls microbes by maintaining temperatures that are too cold for their reproduction. Canning controls microbes by killing them with high temperatures. Dehydration controls microbes by making the environment uninviting for them. Microbes need water to live and multiply. There are some microbes that form spores and hibernate while conditions are too dry, but many microbes will dehydrate and die.

An item doesn't have to be dehydrated until it has absolutely zero moisture in order to be preserved. For example, if you were to dilute some honey with water in a 50/50 ratio, the jar containing the undiluted honey wouldn't spoil, but the diluted honey would. Even though the undiluted honey clearly contains some water, it doesn't contain enough water to support bacterial growth, though the diluted honey will support bacteria like crazy.

So dehydration halts enzymatic processes and deprives microbes of the water they need to live, thereby preventing spoilage.

What Foods Can be Dehydrated?

Any vegetable, fruit, meat, or bread can be dehydrated. The question isn't so much whether it can be dehydrated as whether it makes sense to do so, or how the dehydrated food will be used.

Dehydration does extensive damage to the structural integrity of the cellular walls of foods. As a result, when dehydrated foods are reconstituted by adding water, their consistency is not the same as the fresh product. Canned and frozen foods are very similar to the fresh product, whereas in most cases dehydrated foods will be comparatively mushy or limp. You can dehydrate beef and carrots, but the dehydrated products will go much better in a soup or stew than as a main course of steak.

There are also some practical considerations. In order to be effectively dehydrated, some foods (such as cauliflower) will have to have their cellular walls burst by blanching. Other foods such as apples can be dehydrated just by cutting, dipping in some lemon juice, and putting them in the dehydrator. Yet other foods are almost completely water, such as watermelon. Watermelon contains so much water that dehydrating it would take a long time and all you'd have left at the end would be a vague pink smear.

So even though, in theory, practically any food can be dehydrated, in practice you'll want to reserve dehydration for foods whose value will be enhanced by the process. Dried apples, pears, and bananas, for example, make great snack foods; and if you've ever looked at the prices for prepackaged dehydrating ones, you'll know that making your own dried fruits is clearly financially worthwhile. A tough flank steak cut into strips and dried will be very tender in a stew. Dried onion is a universal spice. Drying homemade bread before it goes bad so you can make your own stuffing mix will save you money at Thanksgiving while providing a superior culinary experience compared to mixes.

It isn't only about dollars and cents, of course. Dehydrated foods can also add an element of convenience. I make a lot of soups and stews during the winter, and it's nice that I can just reach over and grab a handful of dried carrots, dried celery, dried salsify, or even dried red sweet peppers for an addition. When I make my own spaghetti sauces instead of using a commercial thickener, after boiling it down to get the right consistency, I powder some of my dried tomatoes in the blender. They absorb the excess moisture from the sauce while contributing authentic tomato flavor. Drying also concentrates the flavors in food, which is one reason why you use so much less dried basil in a sauce than you would fresh basil.

So you should dry foods that will be useful to you in dried form. Sometimes the range of what would be useful isn't intuitively obvious. You can get some ideas by reading the ingredients on dried salad dressing and soup mixes. Though the first ingredient is usually salt, MSG, or some sort of starch, thereafter you'll invariably find onion, garlic, red bell peppers, peas, and similar old friends. Once you see how dehydrated foods are used, it will quickly become apparent that you can make dehydrated products that are superior to those you can buy.

Steps to Dehydration

Dehydrating food has four steps: preparation, pretreatment, dehydration, and storage. All four steps are important to a properly preserved product, and the details will vary somewhat based upon the specific food.

Preparation involves cleaning or washing, removing seeds or bad spots, and then cutting the food into slices or strips of a uniform thickness between ⅛" and ¼".

Pretreatment methods usually focus on preventing oxidation and breaking down cell walls if that is necessary. In the case of meats, sanitizing the surface by dipping it in a boiling solution is also needed.

Although dehydration can theoretically be practiced by hanging food on racks in the sun, as it is still done in some cultures, for modern schedules you need a dehydrator. You can buy dehydrators at box stores or over the Internet, or you can build your own. The key features you want in a dehydrator are a fan and temperature control.

Once you have dehydrated a food, it will have less moisture than the ambient air, and it will tend to replenish its lost moisture by drawing it from the air. To prevent this, dehydrated foods need to be stored in airtight containers. I use wide-mouthed quart canning jars with sealing lids in most cases, though I sometimes use vacuum sealed bags or airtight plastic containers. These are stored in a cool dark place to prevent damage from sunlight.

Preparation

Few if any foods are improved in quality by any preservation method. In fact, to some degree, the quality of a food that isn't fresh will always suffer. Therefore, you want to start with the best food available. If something is a bit overripe that's okay, and it is fine to trim away any rotten spots so long as you remove them completely. But you don't want to start with food that is clearly past its prime either. Flaccid carrots and wilted celery won't make the best dehydrated vegetables.

The food you start with should be washed in order to reduce bacteria. Just running it under water in the sink and rubbing it dry with a paper towel is sufficient. Over the past decade or so, a lot of people have suffered from food poisoning as a result of commercial farmers carelessly applying raw manure to crops too close to harvest time. The crops have been contaminated with E. coli or other microbes. Likewise, it is almost impossible to assure that no fecal matter has contacted raw meat. So wash it off and blot it dry before starting. If you are processing leafy vegetables, you can dry them adequately using a salad spinner. I picked one up for $10 and I love it.

The food you'll be dehydrating needs to be sliced so that it will dehydrate properly. In general, anything from ⅛" to ¼" is sufficient, but it is important that all of the slices within a batch be pretty much the same thickness. Otherwise, you'll end up with some pieces drying way ahead of others.

Uniform slicing is difficult to accomplish by hand, but there are a number of inexpensive slicing guides on the market that will give you perfectly uniform slices in no time flat. I picked up mine at a big chain pharmacy for $20. It comes with plates for different thicknesses, and it has lasted for years. These work great for fruits and vegetables, but not for meat. In the chapter on building your own dehydrator, I show how you can make your own slicing guide for meats.

Pretreatment

The pretreatment of fruits and soft vegetables amounts to little more than dipping the slices in a solution made from either lemon juice or vitamin C mixed with water. Use 500 mg of vitamin C or two tablespoons of lemon juice per pint of water. These act as antioxidants to avoid drastic color changes from oxygen exposure while the food is drying. Food is perfectly safe if not pretreated with an antioxidant, but it looks more appetizing if it is.

For fruits that are cut in half and will take a long time—more than a day—to dehydrate, they are usually pretreated with either a solution of potassium metabisulfite (the same stuff used in making wine) or sulfured by placing the fruits in an enclosed basket over a mound of sulfur that is set on fire. This is commonly used with apricots, peaches, and nectarines. The sulfur dioxide fumes generated by the burning sulfur combine with water to form an acid that quickly forms sulfites within the fruit. Because I do most of my dehydrating in fall and winter when the house is closed and the smell of burning sulfur is unpleasant, I use potassium metabisulfite in the form of Campden tablets available from home-brewing suppliers. Crush one Campden tablet into a quart of water along with one tablet of vitamin C.

When dealing with vegetables with a tougher cell structure, their pretreatment consists of steam blanching. Examples of vegetables that would need blanching include potatoes, sweet potatoes, carrots, turnips, parsnips, broccoli, cabbage, and salsify. To steam blanch your vegetables after they have been cleaned and sliced, put them in a boiling steamer for 3–4 minutes, then immediately dump them into ice water for another 3–4 minutes. After this, pat them dry, then place them on your dehydrator. Turnips and potatoes would benefit from a dip in lemon juice after blanching to prevent discoloration.

Pretreatment for non-ground meats is accomplished by blanching them in boiling water for just a few seconds until the surface of the meat turns gray. That's enough to kill surface bacteria. There's no need to ice the meat after—just put it right in the dehydrator.

Dehydrating

To dehydrate, you need a dehydrator. Ideally, you want a model with both a fan and a temperature control. The round models you can buy at department stores, such as the Nesco®/American

Harvest®, generally only provide one square foot of space per rack, and they usually include only five racks. These are okay for occasional small batch use, but if you try to use them to put away a half-bushel of potatoes or even a tote of apples, you'll quickly find they are insufficient for the task. Dehydrators of this sort are easy to clean and work very well, and you can find them for as little as $35. So if you have enough space to run three of them at once, you can.

The next level of dehydrator is something like the Excalibur® with fifteen square feet of space, but it carries a rather hefty $270 price tag. If you aren't handy and are short on space, it's still a good option if you expect to do a lot of dehydrating.

A third option is to make your own. In the final chapter of this book I describe a large homemade dehydrator. Depending on how tall you make the racks, you could have 32 square feet of drying space in a dehydrator that costs about $230 to build. That's a lot of dehydrating bang for the buck, so if you are good with hand tools and aren't intimidated by a bit of basic electrical wiring, building your own is the way to go.

Items to be dehydrated are placed in a single layer on the racks without overlapping, the temperature control is set, and the unit is turned on. Though many dehydrators come with books indicating a certain time for dehydrating various items, these times are broad guesses at best. This is because drying time will vary with ambient humidity, thickness of the food, the amount of moisture in the food, and the evenness of the slices. To test if food is done, remove a piece of the dehydrator and allow it to cool. Vegetables are done when hard or crisp. Fruits should be pliable and leathery, but will feel dry and show no moisture if torn and pinched. Dried meats and fish should be tough, but bendable rather than brittle. A bit of oil showing on meats and fish is okay.

The temperature setting is straightforward. Use a temperature between 90 and 100 degrees for herbs, spices, and flowers to protect their flavors. Nuts and seeds should likewise be dried between 90 and 100 degrees to keep their delicate oils from becoming rancid. Fruits and vegetables should be dried at 130 to 140 degrees to protect their vitamin C content, and meats should be dried at 150 to 160 degrees to prevent spoilage while drying.

Storing

It is inevitable that some of the food in the dehydrator will be finished before the rest. As food finishes, take it from the dehydrator and store it in an airtight container. Don't mix different foods in the same container because the flavors will transfer. Keep your containers in a cool place away from light, and keep them sealed when not in use so they don't absorb moisture from the atmosphere. Food will keep this way for up to a year without any trouble.

If you want to keep the food for a very long time, instead of just using an airtight container use one of the many available vacuum sealers, such as the Seal-a-Meal® or the FoodSaver®. Stored this way, even at room temperature, dehydrated food will keep for four or five years. If you want to save them even longer, put your vacuum sealed packages in the bottom of a chest freezer where they will keep for about fifteen years.

An Embarrassment of Riches

I have two dehydrators—a small American Harvest® model that I use for small jobs and a larger homemade model that I use for big harvests. Although the large dehydrator can make huge batches, you'd be surprised how quickly the small batches add to my stash.

We've all had the experience of looking in the refrigerator and realizing that some of the produce that we bought and planned to use is going to go bad before we get to it. When I see that, I just whip out my small dehydrator, slice up the vegetable in question, pretreat it, and pop it in the dehydrator. Even if it is a weeknight. Usually, it's done in the morning and I just put it in a container while getting ready for work. If not, I just let the dehydrator keep running and I don't sweat the fact that it may be overdone before I get home from work. Though it is technically possible to over-dry the food, it is still perfectly usable in soups and stews.

While I only end up doing this once in a while, over time it has added up to quite a stash. These smaller batches of incidental vegetables such as mushrooms added to my larger harvest batches create a comprehensive cabinet of ingredients useful for nearly any meal. Looking in my pantry closet I have several varieties of dried mushrooms (which cost a fortune in the supermarket), dried beets, dried celery, dried lettuce (don't laugh—it gives soups a great flavor!), dried anchovies, dried cabbage, dried tomatoes, dried green and red peppers, dried salsify, dried carrots, and even some homemade instant potatoes. And that barely scratches the surface.

In practice, dehydrating is the simplest and most foolproof method of preserving food, and it takes very little time and effort compared to other methods. It's a perfect method of preserving food for today's busy lifestyles and once you've had a sample of the results, your dehydrator will become one of your favorite tools.

Chapter 2
Dehydrating Fruits

Dried fruit is nature's candy, but unlike candy it retains most of the vitamins, minerals, and fiber inherent in the fruit, making it more nutritious and filling. I adhere to a caveman-style diet, so candy bars are out for me, but dried fruits (in modest quantities) are in. Dried fruits retain the minerals, caloric content, and fiber present in the fresh fruit. They also retain most of the niacin, thiamine, vitamin A, and riboflavin of the fresh fruit. The only vitamin that experiences significant loss during dehydrating is vitamin C, with fruits losing 90% or more of their vitamin C during dehydration. This effect can be ameliorated slightly by choosing to pretreat fruit with ascorbic acid prior to dehydrating.

Dried fruit makes for a healthier sweet snack than most of what you can buy in the snack aisle, but dried fruits (other than raisins) you can buy at the store tend to be so insanely expensive that they are effectively luxury goods. Since I have neither a chauffeur to drop me off at the grocery store in a Rolls-Royce, nor a personal shopper to take care of it for me, I usually make my own dried fruit for a better product at a lower price.

Dried fruits are great plain and also make welcome additions to cereal, fruit and nut mixes, and cake recipes. You can also pulverize dried fruits, mix them with hot water, and reconstitute them into an applesauce-like consistency. A little-known use for dried fruits is in making country wines. Dried fruits contribute sugar, but also lend a distinct and welcome sherry-like character when added during the primary fermentation phase of country wines.

A lot of my dried fruit comes from my apple trees, pear trees, and grapevines out back, but I also buy bananas, pineapples, peaches, and other fruits at the supermarket and farm stands. Sometimes, I buy more than I can use before it goes bad, or I simply have a rough week at work and I'm not home as much as I planned so

I don't eat as much fruit as I expected I would. Either way, I end up with fruit that is going to go bad unless I do something with it. More often than not, that means breaking out the dehydrator.

For apples, I have what must be the world's most nifty invention, though I certainly didn't invent it myself. It is an apple peeler that peels, slices, and cores the apple in seconds. I have a heavy-duty model that has lasted for years. I once had a cheap version, but it broke after using it just a couple of times. For other fruits I end up doing the slicing by hand, but even that way, preparation only takes a couple of minutes.

Selecting Fruit for Dehydration

Any fruit can be dehydrated. The primary question is whether dehydrating that particular fruit will give you an end product you want. Many citrus fruits and some melons contain so much water and so little cellulose structure that dehydrating them gives poor results.

Likewise, the quality of the starting fruit is important. Though I have seen numerous recommendations that only the absolute finest quality fruit be used, that isn't necessary. For example, I have used apples infected with sooty mold (which doesn't penetrate below the skin and is unsightly but harmless) to make spectacular dried apples after peeling off the skin. In such a case, dehydrating gives a very good way to make use of fruits that would otherwise not be palatable. Likewise, bananas that are slightly beyond the fresh-eating stage and turning brown but are otherwise edible are a perfect candidate for dehydrating. By doing this, you are actually adding value.

But it is important that the fruit be sound. By that, I mean it can't be something you wouldn't eat fresh. I would eat the slightly overripe banana without hesitation. And I peeled and ate the apples with sooty mold on the skin. But I wouldn't eat something that was rotting, internally infected with something, or had lost its structural integrity. Since I wouldn't eat those things, I wouldn't dehydrate them either because dehydrating them wouldn't make

them any better. You should also avoid immature fruit. It is best to select ripe or slightly overripe fruit for dehydrating.

Most fruits are good candidates for the dehydrator. Apples, pears, plums, peaches, cherries, bananas, strawberries, and even kiwis can be dehydrated with excellent results.

Preparing Fruit

Fruits with tough or inedible cores should be cored or sliced around the core so it can be discarded. Apples and pears—especially pears—work better when peeled before slicing into ¼" slices. Remove pits for all stone fruits (peaches, cherries, etc.)

It isn't necessary to peel stone fruits, such as plums or nectarines, but they keep better and dehydrate more quickly if they are dipped whole in boiling water for two or three seconds before cutting them in half and removing the stones. Once dipped in boiling water, the skin slips right off if you want to remove it. Stone fruits can be dehydrated as halves with the cut side facing down on the dehydrating tray.

Fruits such as grapes, blueberries, cherries, and figs have a waxy coating that makes dehydrating difficult. You can crack the skins by putting them in a wire basket, immersing them in boiling water for a couple of seconds, and then immersing them in ice water.

After preparation, fruit should be pretreated.

Pretreating Fruit

Fruit is pretreated primarily to inhibit oxidation during drying and storage so it retains its original color, but it has other benefits as well. Pretreatment helps fruits with tough skins, such as grapes, dry more quickly and last longer in storage. It also makes the final product safer by reducing populations of E. coli, salmonella, and listeria.

Pretreatment is accomplished by soaking the prepared fruit in a solution containing lemon juice, citric acid, ascorbic acid (a.k.a. vitamin C), or metabisulfite for five minutes. For apples, pears, cherries, kiwis, bananas, and grapes, I have had best results with vitamin C and citric acid. For stone fruits, such as apricots and plums, I have had best results with sodium metabisulfite.

Type of Solution	Antioxidant Used	Water Used	Cost Relative to Citric Acid
Lemon Juice	2 cups	2 cups	5,340%
Citric Acid	1 teaspoon	1 quart	100%
Ascorbic Acid	2-½ Tablespoons of powdered ascorbic acid	1 quart	950%
Sodium metabisulfite	1 Tablespoon	1 quart	125%

Powdered citric acid, powdered ascorbic acid, and sodium metabisulfite are available inexpensively from suppliers of home-brewing equipment and stores that cater to home-wine makers. In the accompanying table are relative costs for a quart of pretreatment solution for the various options. As you can see, citric acid and metabisulfite are the most cost-effective options, with ascorbic acid as a runner-up and lemon juice being a rather exorbitant approach.

Traditional Sulfuring

Sulfuring has been used in wine making and fruit preservation for centuries. Ancient Romans burned candles infused with sulfur in wine barrels in order to keep them free of spoilage organisms.

The traditional method of sulfuring fruit is to burn the flowers of sulfur (a powdered form of elemental sulfur) in a confined space enclosing the fruit. Damp fruit is stacked on racks and then a hood is placed over the racks. Sulfur is then placed beneath the racks and ignited. The sulfur dioxide fumes produced by the combustion then combine with any moisture present to form a weak sulfurous acid. This acid combines with available sodium and potassium compounds naturally present to form sulfites. The whole process takes only three or four minutes and hundreds of pounds of fruit can be handled at once. The sulfites are both antiseptic and antioxidant.

Though this method works, I don't recommend doing it at home because it is needlessly hazardous. Burning sulfur turns into a molten splattering mass that poses a risk of fire and could easily splash onto skin. Certainly, if you choose to do it done, it should be done outdoors on a rock surface with nothing flammable around.

In addition, the fumes of burning sulfur, if inhaled, will combine with moisture in the lungs to form sulphurous acid[1] and work all manners of harm, similar to the results of inhaling the phosgene from a World War I gas attack. When phosgene gas encounters water in the lungs, it creates hydrogen chloride which combines with water to form hydrochloric acid. As you can imagine, a lung full of hydrochloric acid is a rather dangerous and potentially fatal event. The sulphurous acid created in the lungs from breathing sulfur dioxide is just as dangerous as the hydrochloric acid made by phosgene.

The United States Occupational Safety and Health Administration has established very strict guidelines on exposure to sulfur dioxide because as little as $\frac{1}{10}$ of 1% in a room's atmosphere can kill a person in ten minutes.

This is all a very technical way of saying that even though I have explained how to do sulfuring the old-fashioned way, you shouldn't use this method at home, and certainly not within a dwelling. If you do and you mess up, you could seriously harm or kill yourself or others. Instead, you should use modern sulfiting methods with a strong safety record.

Modern Sulfiting

Sulfites are used ubiquitously in the production of wine and the sanitation of winery and brewing equipment, and they are

---

[1] People are most familiar with Sulfuric Acid, H_2SO_4. Sulfurous Acid is H_2SO_3. Though it is not as strong as sulfuric acid, it is nevertheless insanely dangerous inside vulnerable lung tissue.

commonly used in the production of dried fruit as well as pre-serving kosher sauerkraut. They keep dried fruit from turning brown by inhibiting the enzyme polyphenol oxidase, and by converting ortho-quinones back into diphenols. They've been used in various aspects of fruit processing for over two thousand years.

Despite the long history of sulfite usage, there are reports that some people are sensitive to sulfites and react to them adversely. Attempts to figure out how prevalent this sensitivity may be have given very divergent results ranging from 0.05%[2] of the population through 1%[3] of the population, with about 5% of people with asthma being sensitive. Obviously, if you are sensitive to sulfites, you shouldn't use them as a pretreatment. For everyone else, though, they are an excellent choice with a solid safety record.

Sulfite is generally available in three forms: powdered sodium metabisulfite, powdered potassium metabisulfite, and Campden tablets containing premeasured amounts of either sodium or potassium metabisulfite.

If you are making wine, the difference in atomic weight and taste effects between the sodium and potassium forms of metabisulfite could make a difference in which you choose and how much you use to reach a certain concentration in parts-per-million. But when you are using sulfites for pretreatment of fruits, there is no need to be that precise.

You can mix one tablespoon of either compound (or 40–50 Campden tablets) with one quart of water and swish it around until it is dissolved, then soak fruits in it for five minutes before putting them in the dryer. You can buy two ounces of sodium metabisulfite for $0.99, making it a very cost-effective pretreatment.

---

[2] M.R. Lester, "Sulfite Sensitivity: Significance in Human Health," *Journal of the American College of Nutrition*, 14(3): 229-32.

[3] L.C. Knodel, "Current Issues in Drug Toxicity: Potential Health Hazards of Sulfites," *Toxic Substance Mechanism*, 16(3): 309-311.

Citric Acid/Lemon Juice

Lemon juice will work as an antioxidant for fruits, but you need an awful lot of it as it is mixed with water 50/50 to make an effective pretreatment. Given the cost of lemons and how many it takes to make a cup of lemon juice, it's not a very cost-effective option unless you have a lemon tree, though the fact that it is 100% natural is certainly appealing. If I'm doing some quick dehydrating in a small batch, I'll often squeeze a lemon into a bowl of water and use that.

The active ingredient of lemon juice is citric acid, and citric acid can be purchased in powdered form from home-brewing suppliers and even many major retail websites. It is very inexpensive; you can buy two ounces of citric acid for $2.40. (It's even less expensive on a per-unit basis when purchased in larger quantities.) You mix one teaspoon with a quart of water and pretreat your fruit by soaking it in the solution for five minutes before placing it on the drying rack.

Citric acid is the least expensive pretreatment option for fruits and it works very well on apples, pears, and bananas, among other fruits. Citric acid is what gives lemonade its distinctive taste, and you may notice the taste somewhat in fruits that you treat with it, but that isn't usually a concern. When fruits are dehydrated their sugars are concentrated, so the small amount of acidity imparted from the citric acid remaining on the fruit after it has been soaked is hardly noticeable.

Ascorbic Acid/Vitamin C

Considering the insane prices charged for some vitamin C tablets in stores, you'd think using ascorbic acid as a pretreatment would be cost-prohibitive, but nothing could be further from the truth. Companies selling vitamin C pay for fancy labels, trademarks, marketing campaigns, etc. But when you buy vitamin C powder in a little bag from the home-brewing store, it costs about $3.89 for two ounces (the equivalent of two hundred 500 mg tablets).

On the negative side, you have to use quite a lot of it to make an antioxidant pretreatment. You need 2-½ tablespoons mixed with a quart of water. High concentrations are necessary because it is destroyed by the heat of the dehydrator. Even though vitamin C is a more expensive pretreatment option, if dehydrated fruit will be a major source of vitamin C in your diet, it is worth considering adding it.

Dehydrating

With all the preliminaries out of the way, the actual dehydrating is easy. The three ingredients are temperature, airflow, and time.

Water will migrate from an area where it is more concentrated to someplace where it is less concentrated, assuming that a means for that migration exists. Air can hold more moisture at higher temperatures than it can at lower temperatures. As an extreme example, the amount of moisture necessary to give a relative humidity of 80% at a temperature of 30 degrees will only provide 17% relative humidity at 72 degrees. So the warmer the air, the more quickly and thoroughly it will suck moisture out of the food you are dehydrating.

Of course, you are trying to dehydrate the food rather than cook it, and the higher the temperature used, the more it will adversely affect the vitamin content—especially vitamin C. So the temperatures optimal for dehydrating represent a compromise to achieve the most rapid dehydration without cooking and still retain as many vitamins as possible. The optimal temperature to strike this balance varies with the food being dehydrated, but for fruits it is between 120 and 135 degrees.

Airflow is necessary to expel air that is laden with moisture and bring in fresh air of a lower humidity. In modern dehydrators this is accomplished with a fan, though it can also be done through a "chimney effect" because hot air is lighter than cold air and will naturally rise. So some dehydrators lacking fans have vents in the bottom for fresh air, and vents in the top for warm air to exit. In my experience, fans work more quickly, but I've had success with both designs.

Time is the final ingredient, and the amount of time required depends upon the dehydrating temperature, how thickly the fruit has been sliced, the particular fruit being dehydrated, and the ambient humidity. In practice, this cannot be predicted except in very imprecise terms. It's best to simply keep fruit in the dehydrator and check on it every couple hours until it's done.

Arrange your prepared and pretreated fruit on dryer trays in a single layer with none of the edges touching. This will assure thorough drying. Once the fruit is arranged, put the trays in the dehydrator and turn it on, setting the temperature between 120 and 135 degrees Fahrenheit.

Modern dehydrators provide both heat via an electric heating element and air movement via a fan. Because dehydrating was done throughout most of human history by putting food on racks in the sun, it may seem that modern dehydrators are overkill, but this is not the case. The success of ancient methods of dehydrating was dictated largely by luck: the ambient temperatures and humidity, rainfall, and sunshine. Where I live in New Hampshire, humidity levels during the summer are seldom below 80% and there are times where we don't see the sun for more than an hour or two during the day, so dehydrating on racks in the sun will seldom yield a product that is well preserved and won't mold. In Arizona, traditional methods work much better.

What modern dehydrators give you is the ability to make a product of consistent quality suitable for long-term storage, where the moisture level of the product can be brought well below atmospheric humidity levels in a very short time without mold.

When Is it Done?

With experience, you'll develop an eye for this, but until your eye is developed, here are some ways to test whether fruits are dry enough. Take a piece of the fruit, and tear it in half. Squeeze it as hard as you can near the torn edge. If it shows no evidence of moisture near the tear, it is done. Another indication for most fruits (except for prunes, dates, and raisins) is that they don't stick together. A final test is

to take several pieces while still hot from the dehydrator and put them in a sealed bag (such as a zipper sandwich bag) then pop the bag in the refrigerator. Come back in an hour and see if there is condensation on the inside of the bag. If there is, the fruit needs to be dried longer. If there's no condensation, it is done.

There is no harm, in my opinion, if you over-dry fruit. You know it is over-dried when it is brittle. I find that over-dried fruit is an excellent snack for folks who like crunchy things.

Specific Fruits

Apples and Pears can be peeled or unpeeled. They should be washed and cored. Then they can either be quartered or sliced in ¼" to ⅜" slices and put on the dryer rack after pretreatment. Citric acid works best as a pretreatment for apples and pears. I have a gadget that peels, cores, and slices apples quickly, and I highly recommend getting one if you plan to do a lot of apples.

Melons, including cantaloupe, honeydew, and watermelon, can be successfully dehydrated, but due to their high water content they need to be sliced thickly—into ½" slices—in order to have anything left worth saving! They don't require pretreatment.

Stone Fruits, including cherries, plums, peaches, apricots, and nectarines, need to be washed and pitted. Smaller fruits, such as cherries and apricots, can be halved and placed on the dryer racks, whereas larger fruits should be sliced into ¼" to ⅜" slices. All stone fruits except cherries require pretreatment. Sulfite solution works best, especially for lighter-colored fruits, though a citric acid solution will work if that's all that is available.

Blueberries, Grapes, and Cranberries are unique among fruits in that they will dehydrate best if blanched first. Wash and remove stems, then put them in a fine-meshed rack and dip them into boiling water until you see cracks forming in the skin. Then put them on the drying racks. Grapes will dry better if you cut them in half.

Citrus Fruits, such as lemons, oranges, and grapefruit, can be dried successfully. Lemons and limes can be washed, sliced into ¼" sections, and then dehydrated complete with the skin or rind. Oranges, grapefruit, and other citrus should have the rind removed before sectioning and drying the sections on the racks. Citrus will be brittle when fully dried.

Conditioning

When your fruit is done, it needs to be conditioned prior to final storage. Conditioning is a process of allowing moisture levels to equalize between individual pieces of fruit. In practice, you accomplish this by putting the fruit in an airtight container and letting it sit while sealed for one or two days.

If you notice condensation, put all of the fruit back in the dehydrator for a few hours and try again. Otherwise, after the conditioning period it is ready for long-term storage.

Storage

The gold standard for storing dehydrated fruit is to vacuum seal it and then put it in a chest freezer at 10 degrees or less. Though I have occasionally done this, it makes using the fruit too inconvenient. In my opinion, it is overkill. One of the key advantages of dehydrated foods is that no electricity is required for their preservation, and using electricity to keep them for ten years is overdoing things a bit.

Vacuum sealing is certainly worthwhile for fruit you don't intend to use soon. By evacuating air, you remove both any atmospheric moisture and oxygen. Oxygen accelerates deterioration, hence vacuum sealing enhances the longevity of foods. Vacuum sealer bags are comparatively expensive and they aren't always easy to reseal, so they are best used with items intended to be kept for a long time.

In my opinion, the best way to store dehydrated fruit is in wide-mouthed canning jars. Though the jars admit light and air—both of which hasten deterioration—as long as the jars are kept sealed and in a dark place when not in use, any adverse effects are minimal. Further, the cost savings that accrue through years of reuse combined with the convenience makes them perfect for the job.

Reconstituting Dried Fruit

Most dried fruits are eaten in that form because of their intense sweetness. However, there are cases where rehydrating fruits will be helpful, such as crumbled apple added to oatmeal. In general, fruits rehydrate adequately when mixed with a volume of water roughly equal to the volume of dried fruit. Use room-temperature water, mix thoroughly with the fruit, and let it sit for anywhere from 30 to 45 minutes, stirring occasionally.

Chapter 3
Dehydrating Vegetables

Though fruits and jerky are dehydrated most often, vegetables should not be overlooked. In fact, most of the dehydrated produce in my pantry is constituted of various vegetables. Though I freeze many vegetables, particularly when they will be used as a primary course, dehydrating is far more convenient for vegetables that will be used in soups and stews.

Just as most of the weight of the human body comes from water, most of the weight of vegetables comes from water. Dehydrated vegetables take up far less space than fresh, canned, or frozen ones. Using them is very convenient: just shake a handful out of a jar and put the lid back on. Vegetables tend to lose vitamin C during dehydration and storage, but all the other vitamins and minerals they contain remain intact.

Though there are exceptions, due to the damage to cell walls from the dehydrating process, most dehydrated vegetables don't go well as a standalone vegetable course with dinner. As a blanket statement, this assumes you'd want a reconstituted vegetable to largely resemble the fresh product. However, if that lack of resemblance won't hold you back from trying vegetables with a unique flavor and texture, you'll find that reconstituted vegetables, while decidedly different, are still perfectly delicious assuming you started with a good product in the first place.

Another good use for dehydrated vegetables is as a nutrition booster. When my daughter was a toddler, she loved spaghetti but hated vegetables. So I would powder dehydrated vegetables in the blender and add them to the spaghetti sauce while it was cooking.

Where dehydrated vegetables really shine, though, is in soups, stews, sauces, and dressings. Reading the packages of a number of seasoning mixes for steak and salads, you'll find onion, garlic, red bell pepper, carrots, parsley, lettuce, and celery among other

ingredients. Vegetables, in and of themselves, contribute important flavors to seasoning sauces and dressings. For soups and stews, they will soak up water as they simmer and because their cell walls were damaged during dehydrating, they will release their unique flavors into the soups and stews more readily than even fresh vegetables would.

Selecting Vegetables for Dehydrating

Although it may seem unlikely by looking at some vegetables, such as broccoli, any vegetable can be dehydrated with excellent results provided suitable procedures are followed. Just as with fruits, though most experts say you should only use best-of-the-best vegetables, my experience is that so long as a vegetable is fundamentally sound (i.e. not rotten), it can be enhanced by dehydrating.

A zucchini with a bad spot on it that can't be sold whole as fresh produce can still be dehydrated after the bad spot has been removed. Celery or carrots that have started to go limp in the refrigerator can be blanched and dehydrated with excellent results. While some of my dehydrated vegetable stash comes from items brought in from the garden and processed directly, most of it comes from small batches made from items that were going to go bad in the refrigerator.

Preparing Vegetables

Proper preparation of vegetables is the key element to success in dehydrating them, and the key technique is blanching. The cellular structure of vegetables is far tougher than that of fruits. Blanching helps soften the walls so moisture can be extracted from the cells more readily. It also deactivates enzymes that would otherwise predispose deterioration. With the exception of onions and garlic, all vegetables benefit from blanching.

There are two common forms of blanching: immersion in boiling water, and steam. Both are equally effective. I tend to prefer steam blanching because you lose fewer nutrients from being dissolved

in the water and it's easier to clean up after because I have a steaming pot. On the downside, steam blanching takes twice as long. Vegetables to be dehydrated should be blanched in boiling water for two minutes or steam blanched for four minutes.

When you are blanching vegetables to be frozen, they go straight from the blanching pot into ice water before finally being sealed and frozen. But when you are blanching vegetables to be dehydrated, they go straight from the blanching pot onto the drying racks of your dehydrator.

The other important preparation element is size. Vegetables should be cut into small, uniform pieces before blanching so they can be dehydrated efficiently. Vegetables that can be sliced should be sliced no more than ¼" thick. Vegetables such as broccoli should be cut into chunks no larger than an inch.

Pretreatment of Vegetables

Unlike fruits which are subject to discoloration and browning, most vegetables are more stable so pretreatment isn't necessary following blanching. There are a few exceptions. Though it doesn't affect their quality, onions, salsify, parsnips, potatoes, and some squash tend to brown. If you want to avoid this, pretreatment with either citric acid or sulfite solution as described in the chapter on fruits will suffice.

Dehydrating

Dehydration is accomplished by arranging your prepared and pretreated vegetables on dryer trays in a single layer with none of the edges touching. This will assure thorough drying. Once the vegetables are arranged, put the trays in the dehydrator and turn it on, setting the temperature between 120 and 135 degrees Fahrenheit. You don't want to use temperatures any higher than 135 or the vegetable may "case harden." This means that the vegetable developed a hard outer crust to prevent moisture from escaping

its inner layers; so you are better off on the lower side of that temperature range.

How long it takes depends on how much moisture was in the product in the first place, temperature, humidity, and other factors. Just as with fruits, it isn't the end of the world if they spend too long in the dehydrator, but excessively dried vegetables take longer to rehydrate. Without becoming case hardened, vegetables should be left in the dehydrator until they are brittle or crisp. Because they are so dry, they don't require conditioning like fruits.

Specific Vegetables

Though the preceding information on dehydrating vegetables gives a good overview, some vegetables have specific requirements for best success.

Beets need to be cooked fully, and the skin needs to be removed. Then slice ⅛" thick and dehydrate.

Broccoli and Cauliflower should be cut just as they would be for serving, with any stems halved or quartered before steam blanching.

Brussels Sprouts should be sliced in half, blanched, and placed cut-side-down in the dehydrator.

Cabbage should have outer leaves removed and be sliced ⅛" thick, as if for sauerkraut, before blanching and dehydrating.

Globe Artichokes require special treatment to yield a good product. Slice the hearts ⅛" thick, and boil in a standard citric acid pretreatment solution for six minutes before placing in the dehydrator.

Okra, Parsley, Mushrooms, and Horseradish do not need blanching or pretreatment.

Onions and Garlic need neither pretreatment nor blanching, and they'll be leathery when fully dry. Their pungency transfers to other foods, so don't dry them with other items. Pretreating an onion will help keep it from darkening, but it isn't strictly necessary.

Potatoes work best if fully cooked. Peel, slice into ⅜" slices, and boil them for 20 minutes (in unsalted water) before dehydrating. If you want a less time-consuming method, just bake them in the oven, put them in the refrigerator overnight, and then slice and dehydrate them the next day. Dry until crisp. Potatoes dehydrated this way can be powdered in a good blender and used to make instant mashed potatoes.

Tomatoes, whether ripe or green, don't need pretreatment or blanching. Some people like to remove the skin, and if you want to do this just dip them whole into boiling water in a basket until cracks start to form, then plunge them into ice water. Then the skin slips off easily. Personally, I don't remove the skin. Just slice in uniform slices or small, even wedges, and dehydrate until bordering between leathery and crisp. Powdering dried tomatoes in a good blender makes it easy to reconstitute the tomatoes into tomato paste, or to use them as a thickener in sauces or as a base for tomato soup.

Many people recommend storing dried tomatoes in olive oil. I specifically recommend AGAINST this practice, because botulism spoors can survive dehydrating, and covering the dried tomatoes in oil will exclude oxygen, creating a perfect environment for the development of the botulism toxin. Commercial operations that make dried tomatoes in oil implement very strict acidification protocols in order to assure a pH high enough to inhibit botulism. This isn't practical in a home kitchen.

Storing Dehydrated Vegetables

Dehydrated vegetables need to be stored in a fashion that excludes air so that humidity from the air isn't reabsorbed, and they should

be stored away from light so their colors aren't bleached. I store my dehydrated vegetables in canning jars with an air-tight seal, and in my pantry away from light.

If you are planning to keep the vegetables for a long time, using a vacuum sealer to exclude all oxygen and thoroughly protect the product will increase its lifespan by at least double. If you want to take it to the next level, you can store the vacuum sealed dehydrated vegetables in a freezer. Under those conditions they'll be usable for longer than the human lifespan.

Rehydrating Dehydrated Vegetables

You can rehydrate vegetables by adding boiling water and allowing the mixture to set. The first thing most beginners underestimate is the amount of water required. With the exception of greens, which will rehydrate using one cup of water per cup of dried greens, all other vegetables will require between 2-½ and 3 cups of water per one cup of dehydrated vegetables.

The second thing beginners underestimate is how long it takes vegetables to reabsorb water. Though a few vegetables such as spinach, okra, and sweet potatoes rehydrate in about half an hour, most others will require between an hour and ninety minutes. Once boiling water is added, stir, cover, and go do something else.

Chapter 4
Dehydrating Meat and Fish

Because dehydrating, in a favorable climate, requires no modern technology, dried meats and fish in various forms have formed the backbone of the diets in many traditional cultures for untold centuries. This isn't surprising given that protein is essential for survival, and an ounce of dried meat contains as much as 15 grams of protein.

Dried meat and fish, usually called "jerky," are where you get the most bang for your dehydrating buck. The reason is because most commercial jerky is full of chemicals and sugars, and if you can find jerky without chemicals, you'll have to sell your first-born child to afford it. Drying your own meat and fish will give you an excellent supply of jerky both for snacks and for making instant soups, stews, and stocks on the fly.

True jerky is made by thinly slicing whole-muscle meat, and drying the strips on a dehydrator or in the sun where the climate is conducive. The sliced meat can be marinated, smoked, or rubbed with spices to soak up flavors.

A lot of what is called "jerky" in the supermarket isn't made from whole-muscle meat, it is made from cheap ground meat. One motivation for this is cost, but another is that dried ground meat is easier to chew. One of the downsides is that, for safety reasons, jerky made from ground meat needs to be impregnated with nitrites. In my opinion, the jury is still out on the safety of nitrites[1], so this chapter covers making jerky with whole-muscle meats rather than ground meat.

---

[1] For a more thorough discussion of the positives and negatives of nitrites, please see my book *Modern Caveman*.

Selecting Meat for Jerky

Nearly all commercial jerky in the United States is made from beef, but in theory nearly any meat can be used to make jerky. Other meats present greater risks of parasites and microbes, but these risks can be eliminated with proper preparation and processing. A secondary issue with meats other than beef is that certain meats, poultry in particular, are unappetizing unless cooked in some way before dehydrating.

In general, you want fresh whole-muscle meat that you would ordinarily eat. If you don't usually eat ostrich or rabbit, or you don't like these meats, turning them into jerky won't make them any more appetizing to you.

Meats can come from the supermarket, your backyard livestock, hunting, and various other places. You should be keenly aware of the potential of fecal contamination of the surface of any meat. This is practically certain in the case of fowl because of the way they are processed[2], but it can also occur with deer that has been gut-shot, or anything processed carelessly.

Parasites pose risks as well. The trichinella parasite is common in pork products, as well as bear and raccoon. Recently, it has been reported in ground squirrels. Trichinella can be eliminated by freezing meat in portions no greater than 6" thick at a temperature below 5 degrees Fahrenheit for thirty days. Your typical freezer (such as the one attached to your refrigerator) can't do this, but a good chest freezer can. Double check the temperature in the chest freezer with a thermometer and lower it if necessary.

Hunted meat can have a wide variety of parasites and diseases. Warbles are quite common, and are the larvae of a bot fly. These stay just under the surface of the skin and don't infect the meat, so if the meat is skinned it isn't a problem. Tularemia can be an issue with rabbits and hares. Commercially sold rabbits are tested. If you are hunting rabbit, use gloves and a mask while skinning, and if the liver has white or yellow spots, don't eat the rabbit!

---

[2] For a complete description of processing poultry at home, please see my book *Mini Farming: Self Sufficiency on ¼ Acre.*

Tularemia is sufficiently dangerous to be considered a biological warfare agent.

The biggest concern with larger hunted herbivores, such as deer and Rocky Mountain elk, is Chronic Wasting Disease (CWD). CWD is a prion-based disease similar to "mad cow" disease, and if a human is infected, it can take years to manifest. When it does, the resulting brain damage causes death. So far, transmission to humans has only been demonstrated in a test tube. But given that similar prion diseases in sheep and cattle can be transmitted to humans, and that it can take decades to show signs in a human, caution is in order. If you are a hunter, check with your state's game department to see if you are hunting in an area affected by the disease. If you are, have the meat tested for CWD, and don't use it if it tests positive.

Bovine spongiform encephalopathy (BSE), also known as "mad cow disease" is a more commonly known illness caused by prions. The prions that cause CWD, BSE, and other spongiform enceph-alopathies are not, properly speaking, "alive." They are aberrant proteins that, when introduced into the brain, cause other proteins in the brain to fold in order to mimic them. Viruses, parasites, and bacteria can all be destroyed by sufficient cooking, but prions *cannot* be destroyed by any amount of heat short of their total incineration. That's why you shouldn't eat meat that has tested positive for CWD.

Preparing Meat for Jerky

Once meat has been selected and treated for safety, it should be rinsed in running water, and patted dry with paper towels. Meat will slice more easily if you put it in the freezer for fifteen minutes first. Trim any visible fat, and then slice in strips between ⅛" and ¼" thick. Any length is fine. With red meat, it is usually easy to see the grain of the meat, and if you slice perpendicular to the grain, the jerky will be easier to bite off and chew. Though any truly sharp knife will work, you'll have best results with a ceramic knife and plastic cutting board. Personally, I use a nice carbon-steel blade freshly sharpened.

In theory, you can dehydrate the meat without spicing or using marinade, and I recommend this for jerky that will be powdered later for making "instant stock." But in most cases you'll want to use a marinade because it will allow you to dehydrate at a temperature high enough to kill surface microbes without case hardening the meat. Case hardening happens when the outside dries so quickly that the moisture inside the meat can't get out. Marinating the meat first prevents this.

Marinades

Marinades for jerky have some commonalities with marinades for other purposes, but the nature of jerky means that it should contain no added oils. Vegetable oils in particular shouldn't come into contact with jerky. Minerals such as iron will act as a catalyst to make vegetable oils go rancid. So that they can be kept at room temperature, manufacturers refine vegetable oils to remove any minerals. If you add any vegetable oil to a marinade for jerky, the minerals within the meat, such as iron, will act as a catalyst so the vegetable oil will develop bad flavors over time, and the storage life of the jerky will be shortened dramatically.

Beyond this, there are certain basics that can be elaborated upon with infinite variation. Common to nearly all jerky marinades are soy sauce and liquid smoke. There are many varieties of soy sauce available, but if you are sensitive to gluten you should be sure to choose a gluten-free variety. The salt in soy sauce helps the meat stay preserved longer (so long as you keep it sealed for storage), and doesn't contribute enough sodium to be a medical issue for most people.

Soy sauce contains hydrolyzed soy protein. Though some soy sauces are a true fermented product, most use an industrial process. The soybeans are ground and boiled in a solution of hydrochloric acid then neutralized with lye. This process turns the proteins into free-form amino acids, and the neutralizing results in salt. This is why even soy sauce with no added salt contains a certain amount of it. The glutamic acid formed during hydrolysis imparts a savory flavor, and the salt enhances flavor as well. Gluten-free soy sauce is perfectly fine if you follow a cave-man diet that excludes legumes because the hydrolysis breaks down any problematic proteins.[3]

Liquid smoke is made through what is called "the destructive distillation of wood." It is literally smoke from a wood fire that has been condensed as a liquid and bottled. If you have ever made biochar in a container, the smoke leaving the container is what would be used to make liquid smoke, after ash and solid residues were removed. Anytime wood is burned, a wide array of substances result, including potentially carcinogenic polycyclic aromatic hydrocarbons. But as we well know from traditional bar-becue, smoked hams, and bacon, smoked meat is quite tasty. In the quantities used in making jerky, liquid smoke stays well below the acceptable use limits for carcinogenic compounds.[4] Beyond these two ingredients, marinades will typically include ingredients such as onion powder, garlic powder, Worcestershire sauce, and small quantities of cayenne pepper. But you don't have to limit yourself to these! Meats should be allowed to sit in marinade for anywhere from twenty minutes to six hours in the refrigerator.

Basic Poultry Marinade

½ c.	Soy Sauce
2 Tbsp.	Worcestershire Sauce
1 tsp.	Onion Powder
1 tsp.	Garlic Powder
1 tsp.	Liquid Smoke
½ tsp.	Ground Black Pepper
½ c.	Sugar, Honey, or Maple Syrup (optional)

[3] For more information on problematic proteins in legumes, see my book *Modern Caveman*.

[4] M.D. Guillén, P. Sopelana, and M.A. Partearroyo, "Polycyclic Aromatic Hy-drocarbons in Liquid Smoke Flavorings Obtained from Different Types of Wood. Effect of Storage in Polyethylene Flasks on Their Concentrations," *Journal of Agricultural and Food Chemhistry* 48 (10): 5083–7.

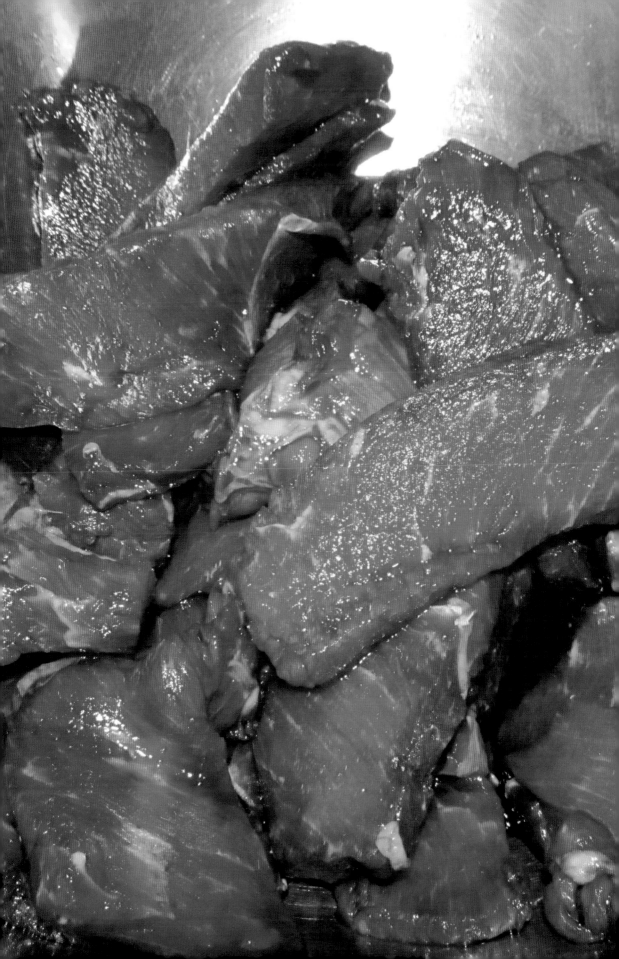

Ginger Poultry Marinade

½ c.	Soy Sauce
1 tsp.	Cider Vinegar
1 tsp.	Garlic Powder
½ tsp.	Ground Ginger
¼ tsp.	Ground Black Pepper

Basic Fish Marinade

½ c .	Soy Sauce
1 tsp.	Liquid Smoke
2 Tbsp.	Lemon Juice
¼ tsp.	Ground Black Pepper
2 Tbsp.	Maple Syrup or Molasses

Teriyaki Fish Marinade

½ c.	Teriyaki Sauce
¼ c.	Water
¼ c.	Sugar or Honey (optional)
2 tsp.	Salt
1 tsp.	Ground Ginger
1 tsp.	Garlic Powder
1 tsp.	Dried Tarragon

Basic Pork Marinade

½ c.	Soy Sauce
1 Tbsp.	Worcestershire Sauce
3 tsp.	Liquid Smoke
1 tsp.	Cider Vinegar
2 Tbsp.	Brown Sugar
⅛ tsp.	Ground Cayenne Pepper

Teriyaki Beef Marinade

½ c.	Soy Sauce
½ c.	Worcestershire Sauce
½ c.	Teriyaki Sauce
2 tsp.	Liquid Smoke
1 Tbsp.	Brown Sugar
2 tsp.	Garlic Powder
2 tsp.	Onion Powder
¼ tsp.	Ground Cayenne Pepper

Basic Beef Marinade

½ c.	Soy Sauce
½ c.	Worcestershire Sauce
1 Tbsp.	Honey
1 tsp.	Ground Black Pepper
1 tsp.	Onion Powder
1 tsp.	Liquid Smoke

Dehydrating

Arrange your prepared and marinated meat strips on dryer trays in a single layer with none of the edges touching. This will assure thorough drying. Once the strips are arranged, put the trays in the dehydrator and turn it on, setting the temperature between 145 and 165 degrees Fahrenheit. If you didn't marinade the meat, stay on the lower end of that temperature range; but in any case use temperatures no lower than 145 degrees Fahrenheit because it is important that the meat attain temperatures throughout that will kill pathogens.

Jerky marinades tend to be very strongly scented, and will affect the flavor of anything else dried at the same time, so jerky should be the only item in the dehydrator.

How long it takes to make jerky depends on how much moisture was in the meat initially, the drying temperature, ambient humidity, and

other factors. Meat should be left in the dehydrator until it is hard to bend (but still bendable), and you see distinct cracks when you bend it.

Conditioning

Like fruit, jerky has enough residual moisture that it needs to be conditioned before final storage. Conditioning is a process that allows moisture levels to equalize between individual pieces of jerky. You accomplish this by putting the jerky in an airtight container and letting it sit while sealed for one or two days.

If you notice condensation, put all of the jerky back in the dehydrator for a few hours and try again. Meat usually contains a bit of fat that may have volatilized during dehydrating, so check whether any condensation you find is water or grease. If it is grease (as evidenced by its slipperiness between the fingers), don't worry about it. Otherwise, put it back in the dehydrator for a while and then repeat the conditioning process. After the conditioning period, your jerky is ready for long-term storage.

Storage

The most certain method for storing jerky is to vacuum seal it and then put it in a chest freezer at 10 degrees or less. Jerky preserved in this fashion will keep for your lifetime, but in my opinion, it is overkill.

Vacuum sealing is certainly good for jerky you don't intend to use soon. By evacuating air, you remove both any atmospheric moisture and oxygen. Oxygen accelerates deterioration, hence vacuum sealing enhances the longevity of foods. Vacuum sealer bags are comparatively expensive and they aren't always easy to reseal, so they are best used with items intended to be kept for a long time.

In my opinion, the best way to store jerky intended for use over the next few months is in wide-mouthed canning jars. Though the jars admit light and air—both of which hasten deterioration—as long as the jars are kept sealed and in a dark place when not in use, any adverse effects are minimal.

Chapter 5
Dehydrating Breads

If you have ever used a prepackaged stuffing mix, bread crumbs, or croutons, you have used dehydrated bread. These items are quite expensive, and often contain ingredients (such as oils in order to make spices stick) that you'd rather not have. It's easy enough to dehydrate bread, but you can go well beyond simple bread by dehydrating cake, pita bread, and other baked goods as well.

Selecting Bread for Dehydrating

Though any bread can be dehydrated, the resulting product will keep better if the proportion of oils (especially vegetable oils) in it is minimal. This is because vegetable oils are highly susceptible to developing off flavors and strange smells when mixed with anything else and left for a while at room temperature. If you are using commercial bread loaves, read the label and make sure the fat content is less than 2 g. per serving.

It is even better if you can make your own bread using a bread machine because when you make your own bread, you can control the ingredients. When making bread intended for dehydrating using a bread machine, if you substitute coconut oil or palm kernel oil for the butter, the keeping qualities of the final product will be greatly enhanced due to the stability of these oils.

Another advantage of using a bread machine is that you can incorporate spices (such as sage and rosemary for fowl stuffing) directly into the bread. In this fashion, you can avoid depending upon added oils to make spices adhere to the dried bread. If you have a bread machine, you already have dozens of recipes in the manual. If you'd like to learn more about baking breads, both using bread machines and using traditional sourdough methods, you'll find a lot of information in my book, *The Mini Farming Guide to Fermenting.*

Cake can also be dehydrated, but just as oils make a difference with the longevity of breads, they also make a difference with cake. For this reason, you are better off making cakes for the purpose of dehydrating. The only commercial cake I've found that is suitable for dehydrating is angel food cake.

Bread Machine Recipes

For both of these recipes, use your bread machine's settings for a 1½ lbs. loaf of white bread, with the crust set to "light."

Stuffing Bread

1 c.	Water (warmed to 80 degrees)
2 Tbsp.	Palm Kernel Oil
2 Tbsp.	Sugar
1-½ tsp.	Salt
2 tsp.	Bell's Poultry Seasoning
1-½ tsp.	Bread Machine Yeast
3 c.	White Bread Flour

Italian Crouton Bread

1 c. + 2 Tbsp.	Water (warmed to 80 degrees)
2 Tbsp.	Palm Kernel Oil
3 Tbsp.	Sugar
1-½ tsp.	Salt
2 tsp.	Dried Italian Seasoning
1-¼ tsp.	Bread-machine Yeast
3-¼ c.	White Bread Flour

Cake Recipes

The key to cake recipes that keep well after dehydrating is the elimination of oils that will go rancid. This includes egg yolk, butter, and unstable polyunsaturated oils that would make them

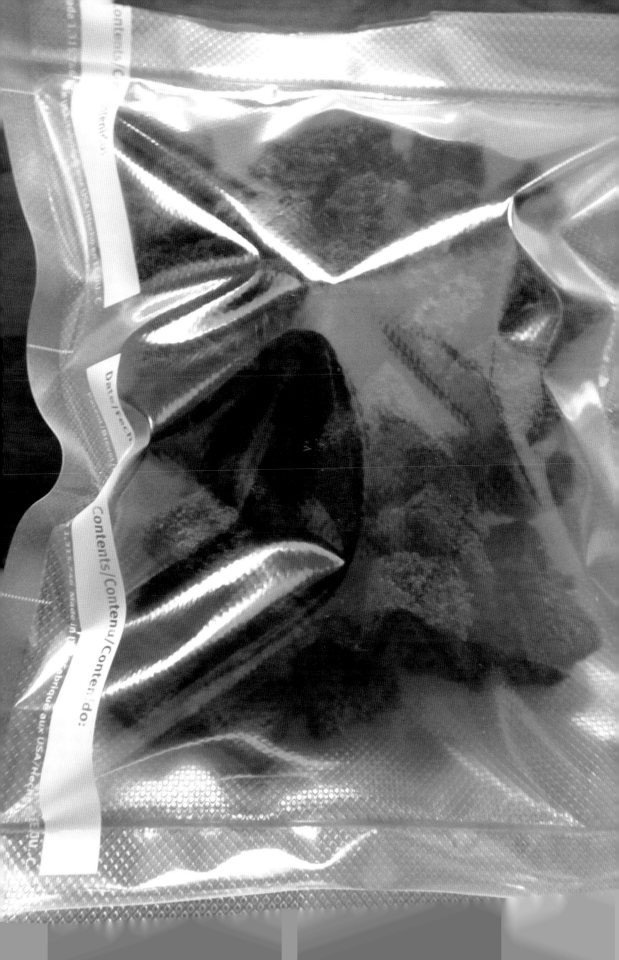

spoil rapidly. You still need a binder, so egg whites or an egg white product such as Egg Beaters™ should be used.

After being baked and cooled, cake should be cut into ½" cubes like croutons before dehydrating. The reason is because this allows the cake to be reconstituted most successfully. To reconstitute dehydrated cake, put one cup of cake cubes in a sealable plastic bag or a bowl, sprinkle in two tablespoons of warm water, and mix carefully. Continue to add water a bit at a time and mix gently until the cake reaches a normal cake-like consistency. This will require between ½ and one cup of water, depending on the particular cake. The taste of reconstituted cake is best when warmed, so you can warm it up in the oven or via a short excursion in the microwave.

Mock Angel Food Cake

2 c.	All-purpose Flour
2-½ tsp.	Baking Powder (Rumford or other non-aluminum powder)
¼ tsp.	Salt
1-½ c.	Sugar
2 tsp.	Vanilla Extract
1 tsp.	Almond Extract
¾ c.	Egg Whites
¾ c.	Nonfat Milk

Real angel food cake achieves leavening through beating egg whites to incorporate air, and then gently folding in the flour. It's a real delicacy when made right! Putting real angel food cake in a dehydrator would be a shame. So I've developed a cake with a similar taste (the secret is the 2:1 ratio of vanilla to almond) that hopefully won't offend culinary sensibilities!

Preheat your oven to 350 degrees. Use palm kernel oil or coconut oil to lightly grease a standard 13 x 9 cake pan. Thoroughly combine the dry ingredients in one bowl and the wet ingredients in another, then combine the wet and dry ingredients thoroughly. Spoon the mixture into your cake pan and place it in the oven. It will take between 30 and 40 minutes to finish. Starting at 30 minutes, test with a toothpick in the center every five minutes until done (when it comes out clean).

Allow the cake to cool on a cooling rack, then dice it into ½" cubes. Dehydrate at 135–145 degrees until hard and crispy.

Egg-Free Chocolate Cake

¾ c.	All-purpose Flour
⅓ c.	Cocoa Powder
2 tsp.	Baking Powder
¼ tsp.	Salt
1 tsp.	Vanilla Extract
⅓ c.	Sugar

Unsweetened Applesauce: Enough to make a thick cake batter, about 1 to 1-½ c.

This recipe is for a small chocolate cake you can make in a small pie tin. Grease the tin using coconut or palm kernel oil. Preheat the oven to 350.

Thoroughly mix the dry ingredients. Then add the applesauce, mixing continuously until you get proper consistency for cake batter. Then add the vanilla extract and incorporate thoroughly. Spoon into the tin, and bake for 25-35 minutes. At 25 minutes, test with a toothpick in the center. If it isn't done (as indicated by the toothpick coming out clean), then continue to bake in five minute increments until done.

Cool the cake on a wire baking rack, then cut into ½" cubes and dehydrate at 135 degrees until crisp throughout.

Storing Dehydrated Breads and Cakes

Dehydrated breads and cakes are fragile and they'll easily turn into crumbs if they aren't packaged and stored carefully. Unlike other dehydrated products, they tend not to shrink very much while drying, so they can also be rather bulky. As with most dehydrated products, wide-mouthed mason jars work well, though you'll want to use the quart size. Another approach is to use vacuum sealer bags, capture as much air in them as you can, and seal them without evacuating the air. This will make the bags into protective balloons. If you were to evacuate the air, the outside pressure would pulverize the bread or cake.

Chapter 6
Dehydrating Herbs and Spices

In the Northeastern United States, most exotic spices, such as cinnamon, nutmeg, and cloves, can't be grown without a prohibitively expensive artificial environment. But a host of herbs commonly used for spicing or herbal tea grow readily. This includes mints, basil, oregano, tarragon, rosemary, chamomile, anise, borage, caraway, dill, thyme, cilantro, fennel, lovage, sage, and summer savory among others. If you are interested in growing your own culinary herbs, I have a chapter dedicated to that subject in my book *The Mini Farming Guide to Vegetable Gardening*. It is very easy to do!

On my mini farm, I have two beds dedicated to growing herbs. I do this because certain herbs, such as lemon verbena, are best used fresh, but also because growing and dehydrating my own herbs for culinary use and teas saves a lot of money. At my local supermarket, just a couple of ounces of dried basil or tarragon costs a fortune. Because I like to use a lot of herbs in my meals, growing and drying my own herbs adds to my bottom line. In addition, the quality of herbs you grow and dry yourself is usually higher. But even more valuable is the fact that I can grow herbs such as savory and lemon balm that are simply unavailable at the grocery store.

Selecting Herbs for Dehydrating

The most important rule for this is the same as the most important rule for what you would grow in a garden or what vegetables you'd dehydrate: only grow and dehydrate herbs that you actually like. It makes sense to experiment a bit with things you've never tried before, just in case you like it. But if you don't like basil, dehydrating a bunch of it is a waste of time.

Generally, you want to harvest herbs during their most vigorous growth and before they set seed so they'll be sweeter. You'll also get more flavor if you harvest them early in the morning before the sun volatilizes the essential oils they've accumulated during the night.

Preparing Herbs for Dehydrating

Herbs need to be washed well before drying because of the myriad birds flying over and rodents running around. Once gathered, herbs should be well-washed in cool running water and then dried gently in a salad spinner. Using cool water helps to preserve the essential oils. Salad spinners are available for $15 or less at major department stores.

Use a pair of sharp scissors to cut the desired part of the herb from the stem. Usually, this will be leaves, though in the case of certain herbs, such as chamomile, it will be flowers. Simply cut the desired part of the plant from the stem, but don't cut up leaves or flowers any further.

Dehydrating Herbs

The active principles of herbs are usually, though not always, essential oils that can be easily driven away by excess heat. Even with herbs whose flavor is primary a result of nonvolatile components, excess heat will often cause them to be bitter. Therefore, herbs should be dried at temperatures not exceeding 115 degrees Fahrenheit. Place herbs on a fine-meshed screen in the dehydrator, and leave until they are crisp.

Storing Herbs

Although the bottles of herbs you'll find in the grocery store are usually finely chopped or ground, that is the last thing you want to do to an herb until the very minute it is used. For purposes of storage, herbs should be kept as intact as possible. The reason is because chopping or grinding the dried herb exposes far more

surface area which will simultaneously allow more of the flavoring compounds to escape, while diminishing flavor of the components that remain through oxidation. So the desired parts of herbs should be stored in a form that is as intact as practical.

Herbs are best chopped, ground, or powdered immediately before use. If you've ever compared freshly milled pepper from a pepper mill to that from a can in the grocery store, you'll see a tremendous difference. The same difference applies to any herb or spice.

Being delicate, dried herbs should be stored in a rigid container for protection. Vacuum sealing isn't practical because it would turn dried herbs to dust. You also want to store herbs so that there is as little room for oxygen as possible. So I recommend using the smallest canning jars available, which are typically 8 ounce or ½ pint jars. Sunlight wreaks havoc on herbs, so store them away from the sun. Heat can cause undesired changes in flavor as well as loss of flavor components, so also store them in a cool place.

Chapter 7
Making "Instant" Foods

Modern lifestyles don't leave people with a lot of time, especially during the work week. In practice, this results in a great many meals being eaten out at restaurants, fast food, and on-the-go meals. Dehydrating allows you to invest the time when you have it on a weekend, and reap the benefit through time savings throughout the week.

There are a lot of ways to do this. My family does once-a-week cooking, where a number of dishes are made over the weekend, stored in the freezer, and then popped into the microwave for lunches and dinners over the course of the week. Over time, we build a supply of one-dish meals, such as baked stuffed peppers and shepherd's pie, and we also store individual entrées and side dishes that can be mixed and matched.

Dehydrated foods can also help with this generally, because all of the work of harvesting and cutting has already been done. If you are making a stew and need some carrots, you don't have to get out a cutting board and knife. (And you won't need to wash them.) Instead, pour a cup of dehydrated carrots into your stew.

But dehydrated foods can go well beyond this, into the realm of nearly instant foods. If you have ever tried a cup of ramen noodles or some packaged instant soup, you've certainly noticed that the ingredients are dehydrated. You'll also find that instant salad dressing mixes, instant flavored oatmeal, and many other convenience foods are little more than precooked dehydrated ingredients.

Principles of Instant Foods

Foods intended for instant use are precooked whenever they would usually need cooking to be consumed. For example, if you want to include broccoli, peas, and carrots in an instant food, these would all be precooked before dehydrating, rather than merely blanched. Apples wouldn't need to be precooked because apples are usually eaten raw, though if you wanted to make instant applesauce you would cook them slightly before dehydrating.

The other principle is that of fine division. That is, anything you expect to rehydrate quickly will have to be as small as possible. Pre-cooked potatoes intended for use as instant mashed potatoes would be powdered in a blender after dehydrating so that they rehydrate more quickly. If you plan to make an apple-flavored instant oat-meal mix, then the pieces of apple included should be small.

The final principle is that of pre-combination. As with the stuffing-bread recipe in Chapter 5, in which the spices are baked into the product, dry ingredients of instant food are combined together and then packaged. Because the ingredients are dried and sealed, they won't intermingle until water is added, and the resulting conve-nience makes them a time-saver.

Instant Mashed Potatoes

Peel potatoes, cut in ¼" slices, and boil until tender. Using a slot-ted spoon to drain excess water, put the potato slices in the dehy-drator to dry. Dry at 135 degrees until rock-hard. Put the slices in a blender, and pulverize into as fine a powder as the blender will make. Store in portions suitable for your family in vacuum sealed bags until ready for use.

To reconstitute, combine two cups of wet ingredient (boiling in a pan) for every 1-⅓ cups of dry ingredient. The reason I specified it this vaguely is because a lot of people love milk in their mashed potatoes whereas others are lactose intolerant. Many people love butter in their mashed potatoes, but some people are on a diet that restricts it. Your two cups of wet ingredients can be composed of any combination of water, milk, butter, or other fat. So you can use 1 cup of water and 1 cup of skim milk if you are on a fat-free diet, or you can use 1-¾ cups of water and a half stick of butter (which equals a quarter cup) if you are lactose intolerant. Because batches will vary a bit, the amount of liquid you need will vary. Start with ¾ths of the liquid, and then add a bit at a time until the desired consistency is reached. Most people find flavor is enhanced by adding up to ½ tsp. of salt per two cups of liquid ingredients.

The same technique used here can also be used with sweet potatoes, yams, turnips, winter squash, and any other vegetable usually served mashed.

Bouillon

Bouillon is used as a base for soups and broths. Most bouillon you can find in the store is composed primarily of either salt or mono-sodium glutamate (MSG) with only a hint of real flavor. You can make your own bouillon from jerky, and it is dramatically better.

Jerky used for making bouillon should be marinated for a few hours before dehydrating using one of the basic marinade recipes in the chapter on meats and fish. Then it is dehydrated for an additional twelve hours after it would ordinarily be considered done. This will make it hard as a rock. Now, powder it in a high-quality food processor. One rounded teaspoon of this powder will make one cup of broth or stock.

For an even better bouillon, powder some dehydrated celery, onion, and sweet pepper. Mix this with the powdered jerky in a ratio of ⅓ vegetable to ⅔ jerky.

Bouillon made this way needs to be well-sealed so it won't go bad by drawing moisture from the air. But as long as you keep it sealed when not in use, it will last years.

Vegetable Soup

Vegetable soup needs a base for flavor combined with some solid ingredients. The flavor base is composed of powdered onion and powdered celery in a 2:1 ratio, and the solid ingredients are composed of small chunks of dehydrated vegetables such as tomato, pepper, and carrot. Salt is commonly present as a flavor enhancer.

Instant Vegetable Soup (This is just one example.)

1 tsp.	Powdered Onion
½ tsp.	Powdered Celery
½ tsp.	Salt
1 Tbsp.	Dehydrated Red Sweet Pepper, coarsely chopped
1 Tbsp.	Dehydrated Carrot, coarsely chopped
1 tsp.	Dehydrated Tomato, coarsely chopped

Store in an airtight package until ready for use. This recipe can be multiplied as many times as you'd like. Add one cup of boiling water to 3 tablespoons of instant vegetable soup mix. Stir, and allow to stand five minutes before enjoying.

Instant Tomato Paste

If you've ever tried to make home-canned spaghetti sauce, you've likely been frustrated at being unable to get it as thick as commercial sauces. Commercial sauces can be thickened without burning because excess water is removed via a vacuum process that can't readily be duplicated on a home-scale. Thickeners such as flour or corn starch shouldn't be used in canning because they can make a product that isn't properly preserved. The solution lies in the perfect thickener: powdered dehydrated tomatoes.

Dehydrate tomatoes as directed in the chapter on dehydrating vegetables, except dry them until they are crisp. Allow them to cool, then put them in a food processor and turn them into powder. Store the powder in an airtight container away from light and heat.

Instant tomato paste can be used to make tomato paste by mixing it with hot water a little at a time until the desired consistency is achieved. When used as a thickener in sauces, it will absorb three times its volume of water.

You could also use this to make tomato soup, but if used for that purpose, mix it with powdered onion and powdered celery in a ratio of 5 parts tomato to 2 parts onion to 1 part celery by volume. To make tomato soup, add one cup of boiling water to ⅓ cup of this mixture, stir, and allow to sit covered for five minutes.

Instant Oatmeal

The individual packets of instant oatmeal at the supermarket are ridiculously expensive compared to the retail cost of their raw ingredients. You can save a lot of money by purchasing the big round containers of instant oatmeal, and then adding your own ingredients to make single-serving bags using resealable sandwich bags.

Looking at the ingredients and nutrition label of a popular "apples and cinnamon" variety of instant oatmeal, it becomes clear that fully one-third of the weight of the product is sugar, a negligible amount is provided by the cinnamon and dehydrated apples, and the balance is oatmeal.

To make your own far superior product, combine the following for a single serving:

- ⅓ c.   Instant Oatmeal
- ⅓ c.   Dried Fruit
- 1 Tbsp.   Sugar (less if desired)
- Any spices you desire

The dried fruit should be broken up into small chunks no larger in any dimension than ¼" so it rehydrates easily. To use, put your mix in a bowl and add between ⅔ and one cup of boiling water. Stir and allow to sit covered for a few minutes.

Instant Salad Dressings

I eat a lot of salad, but I don't like premade salad dressings because so many of them contain non-food ingredients. Examples of non-food ingredients I've seen on labels of salad dressings include propylene glycol (a safe antifreeze), disodium inosinate, disodium guanylate, FD&C Blue 1 Aluminum Lake, etc.

The dry mixes are a bit better, but with their most dominant ingredients being sugar, salt, and MSG, they aren't worth their cost. It's far better to make your own. The primary advantage of the mixes from the grocery store are that they contain guar gum, xanthan gum, and similar ingredients that help the oil and vinegar

mix. But if you don't mind shaking your dressing before pouring, you've lost nothing and gained much by making your own.

Instant Italian Dressing Mix

1 Tbsp.	Sugar
1 Tbsp.	Salt
1 tsp.	Garlic Powder
1 Tbsp.	Onion Powder
¼ tsp.	Celery Seed
½ tsp.	Dehydrated Red Pepper, broken up fine
1 Tbsp.	Dried Oregano
1 Tbsp.	Dried Parsley
1 tsp.	Dried Basil
½ tsp.	Black Pepper Flakes
½ tsp.	Thyme

The above recipe makes a little more than enough for three batches, so feel free to multiply it as needed. Store in an airtight container in a cool place away from sunlight. To turn this into Italian dressing, mix two level tablespoons with ⅔ cup olive oil, ¼ cup vinegar, and two tablespoons of water. Shake vigorously, and then shake just before using.

Chapter 8
Recipes

Bread Machine Breads for Dehydrating

The following recipes are for a 1-½ lbs. loaf. Put the water in the bottom of the pan, add the mixed dry ingredients (except yeast) to the bread pan, evenly distribute any fats into four corners of the bread pan, and then put the yeast in the very center of the dry ingredients. Water should be heated to approximately 90 degrees before adding to the pan. Follow the directions for your bread machine to make a 1-½ lbs. loaf with a lightly browned crust.

Dill Bread

1-¼ c.	Water (warmed to 90 degrees)
2 Tbsp.	Palm Kernel Oil
2 Tbsp.	Sugar
1-¼ tsp.	Salt
1 Tbsp.	Dried Dill Weed
2 Tbsp.	Non-fat Dry Milk
1-½ tsp.	Bread-machine Yeast
3-½ c.	White Bread Flour

Rosemary Bread

1 c.	Water (warmed to 90 degrees)
2 Tbsp.	Palm Kernel Oil
2 Tbsp.	Sugar
1-½ tsp.	Salt
¼ tsp.	Dried Italian Seasoning
¼ tsp.	Ground Black Pepper
2 tsp.	Powdered Rosemary
1-½ tsp.	Bread-machine Yeast
2 -½ c.	White Bread Flour

Herbed Bread

1 c.	Water (warmed to 90 degrees)
2 Tbsp.	Sugar
2 Tbsp.	Palm Kernel Oil
3 Tbsp.	Nonfat Dry Milk Powder
1-½ tsp.	Dried Basil
1-½ tsp.	Dried Dill
1 tsp.	Onion Powder
1-½ tsp.	Garlic Powder
3 c.	Bread Flour
1-½ tsp.	Bread Machine Yeast

Cakes for Dehydrating

Plain Vanilla Cake

2 c.	All-Purpose Flour
2 tsp.	Baking Powder (Rumford or other non-aluminum powder)
1 tsp.	Baking Soda
¼ tsp.	Salt
1 c.	Sugar
1 c.	Unsweetened Applesauce
1 tsp.	Vanilla Extract
¾ c.	Egg Whites
¾ c.	Nonfat Milk

Preheat your oven to 350 degrees. Use palm kernel oil or coconut oil to lightly grease a standard 13 x 9 cake pan. Thoroughly combine the dry ingredients in one bowl and the wet ingredients in another. Once the oven is preheated, combine the wet and dry ingredients thoroughly, then spoon the mixture into your cake pan and place it in the oven. It will take between 30 and 40 minutes to finish. Starting at 30 minutes, test with a toothpick in the center every five minutes until done (when it comes out clean).

Allow the cake to cool on a cooling rack, then dice it into ½" cubes. Dehydrate at 135–145 degrees until hard and crispy.

Chocolate Cake

3-⅓ c.	All-purpose Flour
2 c.	Cocoa Powder
3 tsp.	Baking Soda
2 tsp.	Salt
1 c.	Egg Whites or Egg Beaters™
2 Tbsp.	Vanilla Extract
2 c.	Sugar
3 c.	Fat-free Sour Cream or Fat-free/sugar-free plain yogurt
1 c.	Unsweetened Applesauce

This recipe is for a pretty large batch of cake, so you can cut the proportions in half if needed. It is intended for use with two 13 x 9 glass baking pans. As with bread recipes, it is important that the dry ingredients for this recipe be measured properly. Use a set of dry measuring cups. Spoon the dry ingredient into the cup until it is overflowing. Do NOT pack. Do NOT just scoop the ingredient directly into the cup. If you do, it will cause compaction and throw off the proportions. After the dry measure is overflowing, use the straight back of a kitchen knife to remove the excess.

This recipe will stick to baking pans with a vengeance. To avoid this problem, grease the pan using coconut or palm kernel oil, insert a piece of wax paper cut to fit the pan, and then lightly grease the wax paper before adding the ingredients.

Preheat the oven to 350. Thoroughly mix the dry and wet ingredients separately, then mix the wet and dry ingredients together just enough to make sure everything is well moistened and incorporated. Pour into the pans, and bake for 30–40 minutes. At 30 minutes, test with a toothpick in the center. If it isn't done (as indicated by the toothpick coming out clean), then continue to bake in five minute increments until done.

Cool the cake on a wire baking rack, then cut into ½" cubes and dehydrate at 135 degrees until crisp throughout.

Instant Salad Dressings

Instant Zesty Italian Dressing Mix

1 Tbsp.	Sugar
1 Tbsp.	Salt
1 tsp.	Garlic Powder
1 tsp.	Onion Powder
½ tsp.	Dehydrated Red Pepper, broken up fine
1 tsp.	Dried Oregano
1 tsp.	Dried Basil
½ tsp.	Black Pepper Flakes
¼ tsp.	Cayenne pepper powder

The above recipe makes a little more than enough for three batches, so feel free to multiply it as needed. Store in an airtight container in a cool place away from sunlight. To turn this into Italian dressing, mix two level tablespoons with ⅔ cup olive oil, ¼ cup vinegar and two tablespoons of water. Shake vigorously, and then shake just before using.

Dried Tomato Dressing

1 c.	Dried Tomatoes
1 tsp.	Dried Basil
1 tsp.	Garlic Powder
½ c.	Water
3 Tbsp.	Balsamic Vinegar
⅔ c.	Olive Oil

Add all of the ingredients except the oil to a blender, and blend until smooth. Add the olive oil slowly while blending. Serve fresh! NOTE: Due to low vinegar content this dressing shouldn't be stored in the refrigerator for more than seven days.

Soups

Meat Bouillon

8 oz.	Well-marinated jerky, dried until extra-hard
½ c.	Dried Onion

½ c.   Dried Celery
¼ c.   Dried Sweet Pepper

This recipe works for any type of meat or fish. You'll need a very good food processor/blender. Break up the jerky into pieces no more than one inch long, and process into a powder in the food processor. Add the dried onion, celery, and sweet pepper, reducing those to powder too. Mix thoroughly, and store in an airtight container away from heat and light.

Vegetable Bouillon
½ c.   Dried Celery
½ c.   Dried Onion
¼ c.   Dried Carrot
¼ c.   Dried Red Sweet Pepper
½ tsp.   Salt
1 tsp.   Garlic Powder
¼ tsp.   Black Pepper

Put all of the ingredients into a food processor and blend into a powder. Store in an airtight container in a dark place. Use 1-½ tsp. bouillon per cup of water to make vegetable stock.

Mushroom Soup
1-½ c.   Dried Mushrooms
½ c.   Dried Onions
2 tsp.   Powdered Beef Bouillon
1 tsp.   Salt
¼ c.   Butter
4 c.   Water

Heat two cups of water to boiling in a saucepan, remove from heat, and add the dried mushrooms and onions. Allow to sit five minutes. Heat butter in a pan over low-medium heat, remove the mushroom and onion from the water with a slotted spoon, and sauté the mushrooms and onions in the butter, reserving the liquid in which they were soaked. Add two more cups of water, the powdered beef bouillon, and the sautéed onions and mushrooms back to the saucepan. Put the saucepan back on the burner, bring to a boil, then reduce heat and allow to simmer, stirring occasionally, for fifteen minutes before serving.

Vegetable Noodle Soup

4 c.	Water
6 tsp.	Vegetable Bouillon (from recipe in this chapter)
½ c.	Dried Carrots
¼ c.	Dried Onions
1 clove	Garlic, sliced small
½ c.	Potatoes, dried and cubed
1 c.	Fresh Cabbage, sliced fine
1 c.	Dried Egg Noodles
½ tsp.	Oregano
½ tsp.	Basil
2 Tbsp.	Olive Oil
To taste	Salt and Pepper

Bring olive oil to medium heat in a frying pan, and sauté the cabbage and garlic together until the cabbage is well-wilted. Combine all ingredients (including the cabbage and garlic from the previous step) in a medium sauce pan. Bring to a boil, stirring occasionally, then reduce heat and simmer until the noodles are done.

Beef Jerky Soup

8 oz.	Beef Jerky, broken or cut with scissors into small chunks
3 c.	Water
1 c.	Red Wine (not cooking wine—use the real thing!)
2 tsp.	Vegetable Bouillon (recipe earlier)
1 tsp.	Beef Bouillon (recipe earlier)

Simmer on the stove for up to two hours until the beef is tender. Then add the following:

½ c.	Dehydrated Potato Cubes
½ c.	Dehydrated Carrots
¼ c.	Dehydrated Onion
¼ c.	Dehydrated Celery
½ tsp.	Garlic Powder
½ tsp.	Oregano
½ tsp.	Dried Basil
½ tsp.	Dried Thyme

Simmer for an additional 30 minutes until all is tender and melded. Serve hot.

Onion Soup

1 c.	Dried Onion Pieces
½ c.	Beef Bouillon Powder (from earlier recipe)
2 Tbsp.	Onion Powder
1 tsp.	Ground Black Pepper

Combine dry ingredients and store in an airtight container away from light. To make onion soup, combine three tablespoons of the mix with eight ounces of boiling water, allow to stand covered for a few minutes then enjoy.

Instant Vegetable Soup

1 tsp.	Powdered Onion
½ tsp.	Powdered Celery
½ tsp.	Salt
1 Tbsp	Dehydrated Red Sweet Pepper, coarsely chopped
1 Tbsp.	Dehydrated Carrot, coarsely chopped
1 tsp.	Dehydrated Tomato, coarsely chopped

Store in an airtight package until ready for use. This recipe can be multiplied as many times as you'd like. Add one cup of boiling water to 3 tablespoons of instant vegetable soup mix. Stir, and allow to stand five minutes before enjoying.

Trail Mixes

Tropical Mix

1 c.	Dried Coconut Flakes
½ c.	Dried Pineapple
½ c.	Dried Mangoes or Dried Apricots

Cut all pieces no larger than ½" in any dimension. Mix thoroughly. Store in an airtight container away from sunlight.

Fruit and Nut Mix

1 c.	Dried Apples
½ c.	Dried Grapes (Raisins)
½ c.	Dried Plums (Prunes)
½ c.	Dried Bananas
½ c.	Pecans, Broken
¼ c.	Pistachios

Cut the apples and prunes in pieces no larger than ½" in any dimension. Break up intact pecans slightly. Shell pistachios if needed. Mix thoroughly and store in an airtight container away from sunlight.

Sinfully Sweet Mix

1 c.	Dried Apples
½ c.	Dried Grapes (Raisins)
½ c.	Bittersweet Chocolate Chips
½ c.	Almonds

Break up the almonds slightly, cut the apples in pieces so they're no larger than ½" in any dimension. Mix thoroughly. Store in an airtight container in a cool, dry place, away from sunlight.

Kid's Delight

½ c.	Dried Apples
½ c.	Dried Bananas
½ c.	Dried Pineapple

Break, tear, or cut pieces so they are no larger than ½" in any dimension. Mix thoroughly, then store in an airtight container away from sunlight.

High Protein Mix

½ c.	Beef Jerky
¼ c.	Raisins
¼ c.	Pumpkin Seeds
Pinch	Dried Seaweed, cut or crumbled

The jerky is a bit salty, the raisins are sweet, and the seaweed acts as a flavor enhancer, so this is surprisingly tasty despite the unusual ingredients. Cut the beef jerky in pieces no larger than ½" in any dimension. Add raisins and pumpkin seeds, then sprinkle with some cut or crumbled dried seaweed. Mix thoroughly. Store in an airtight container away from sunlight.

Special Snacks

Raw Kale Chips

2 lbs.	Kale or Swiss Chard
½ tsp.	Celtic Sea Salt
1	Lemon
½ tsp.	Garlic Powder
2 Tbsp.	Olive Oil
1 tsp.	Toasted Sesame Seed Oil

Most people prefer kale for this recipe, but I prefer Swiss chard as it agrees better with my digestion. Remove large ribs from the kale and cut it into strips. (I find scissors work best.) Put the strips in a large bowl. Rapidly mix the oils, the juice from the lemon, the salt, and the garlic powder in a separate bowl, then pour the mixture over the kale and work it into the kale thoroughly with your hands, so it is completely covered. Lay the strips on the dehydrator trays, and run the dehydrator at 145 degrees until the strips are crunchy. Carefully gather and store them in an airtight container. This will keep for two weeks.

Cinnamon Apple Crisps

12	Apples (I prefer Granny Smith, but any kind will work)
1 tsp.	Ground Cinnamon
¼ c.	Honey
1	Lemon
Nonstick Cooking Spray	

The secret to making dehydrated apples crisp and crunchy is to slice them thinly. I use what is called a "mandolin slicer" with an insert gauged for ⅛". Peel and core the apples, then slice them into ⅛" slices. Put the apples in a large bowl. Spray a bit of nonstick cooking spray into a measuring cup and distribute it evenly, then add the honey to the measuring cup. Squeeze the juice of one lemon into the measuring cup.

Put the cup in the microwave for ten seconds at a time until the honey is runny. Then stir in the cinnamon. Pour the mixture over the sliced apples, and use clean hands to coat them with the mixture as uniformly as practicable. Spray the dehydrator trays lightly with nonstick cooking spray. (If you don't, the honey will make these stick to the trays like glue.) Place the coated apple slices on the dehydrator trays without overlap, and dehydrate at 150 degrees until crisp. Store in an airtight container away from sunlight. These will keep for about a month.

Candied Fruit

Fruit of choice, cut
1 c.   Sugar
1 c.   Honey
1½ c.   Water
Non-Stick Cooking Spray

Cut fruits into pieces no larger than ½". Cut berries, grapes, and similar fruits in half.

Combine the sugar, honey, and water in a heavy saucepan, and heat on medium heat until the temperature reaches 235 degrees on a candy thermometer. Maintain temperature as close to 235 degrees as you can throughout the process.

Add ½ c. of fruit to the syrup, and allow it to boil until it is transparent at the edges, which will take between 10 and 20 minutes, depending on the fruit.

Use a slotted spoon to remove the fruit, and spread it on a dehydrator tray that has been sprayed with nonstick cooking spray.

Add the next batch of fruit to the syrup, and repeat the process until all the fruit is on the dehydrator trays. Dehydrate at 135 degrees until leathery and a piece of fruit torn in half and squeezed shows no moisture. Will keep indefinitely in an airtight container.

Variation: Add 1 tsp. Ground Cinnamon, ½ tsp. Ground Cloves, and ½ tsp. Allspice to the syrup.

Cinnamon Banana Crunchers

6   Bananas, just ripe but not over-ripe
¼ c.   Honey
½   Lemon
½ tsp.   Ground Cinnamon
Nonstick cooking spray

As with the last recipe, the secret to crunchy bananas is to slice them thinly, no more than ⅛" thick. If you slice them any thicker, they'll be like rocks and will break instead of crunch. Bananas are too delicate for a mandolin slicer, so I just do it by eye. If you aren't familiar with measurements like this, just look at a ruler to see how thick ⅛" is.

Slice the bananas thinly and put them in a medium bowl. Lightly spray the inside of a measuring cup with nonstick cooking spray, then add the honey to the cup. Squeeze ½ of a lemon into the cup as well. Heat the measuring cup in the microwave for 10 seconds at a time until the honey is runny, then stir in the cinnamon.

Pour the mixture over the bananas, then use your clean hands to carefully make sure the banana slices are fully coated. Then lightly spray the dehydrator trays with nonstick cooking spray, and put the banana slices on the trays without overlapping. Dehydrate at 135 degrees until crispy. Store in an airtight container for up to two weeks.

Summer Squash Crunchy Surprise

> Summer Squash (and/or Zucchini)
> Celtic Sea Salt
> Freshly Ground Black Pepper
> Melted Coconut Oil

If you've ever grown summer squash and planted too many plants, you know what I mean by "Summer Squash Surprise!" The yield is so impressive that it's hard to know what to do with it all! Well, here's an idea: turn your excess into crunchy chips! A bonus is that a friend of mine keeps wanting a chip that can be used with dips, and is also paleo diet friendly.

The amount of each ingredient depends on how much squash (or zucchini) you have, and your taste preferences. As with the other recipes in this section, the key is to thinly slice the squash (or zucchini). Use a mandolin slicer to cut your squash into uniform ⅛" slices. Put the slices in a large bowl, pour some melted coconut oil over them, and use your clean hands to uniformly and lightly coat the squash slices. Then add finely ground sea salt and freshly ground black pepper, again using your clean hands to thoroughly distribute the salt and pepper.

Place the slices on the dehydrator trays, and dehydrate at 135 degrees until crispy. Coconut oil is stable, so you can store these in an airtight container at room temperature for up to a month.

Green Bean Crunchers

Green Beans
Celtic Sea Salt
Melted Coconut Oil

Green beans make an excellent crunchy snack. Steam blanch them for five minutes, immerse them in ice water, and then dump them on some clean, fluffy bath towels to pat off all the water. Put in a large bowl, and use your clean hands to distribute coconut oil lightly and uniformly among the beans. Then add fine sea salt and distribute.

Put the beans on the dehydrator trays, and dehydrate at 135 degrees until crisp. These will keep in an airtight container for up to a month.

Chapter 9
Build Your Own Dehydrator

My father taught me about a million useful things. When I was a kid, I'd keep him company and hand him tools or help him measure things while he was doing home repairs, fixing cars, building chicken coops, plumbing, rewiring old houses and hundreds of other projects. Hardly a day goes by when I don't use some skill I learned from helping and observing my dad.

One thing I learned is that when you build something yourself, it is generally better than something you can buy. It may or may not be cheaper, but it will be better.

I have two dehydrators that can be purchased at a hardware or department store. They are very nice, and I use them for quick jobs and small batches. But because they are small, they only hold about five square feet. And because they are round, only about four square feet of that is usable. This makes them unsuitable for larger jobs, such as dehydrating several pounds of tomatoes.

I looked on the Internet, and I found some decent larger dehydrators, but they were pretty expensive. The one I designed for this book costs about $200 to build, holds 16 square feet as-built, and can be expanded to hold up to 28 square feet just by making additional inexpensive trays. That is very good bang for your buck!

This project requires skills in measuring and cutting lumber as well as electrical wiring. For people with these skills, it is a very minor task. But if you lack these skills, you'll need to find someone who has them and have them help you. If you have no idea how the electricity in your wall sockets works, do not undertake this project alone! Likewise, if you are unfamiliar with the operation of power tools, seek guidance as power tools are quite dangerous if used unsafely.

Materials

6	2" x 2" pieces of ⅜" finished plywood
4	1" x 2" lumber, 23-¾" long
4	1" x 2" lumber, 19-⅞" long
3	1" x 2" lumber, 22-¼" long
1	1" x 3" lumber, 22-¼" long
2	1-¼" height x 1-¼" width lumber, 18" long
6	¾" plastic round corner molding, 22" long
12	1-½" x ¾" plastic molding, 22-¼" long (on the long edge), ends cut at 45 degrees using a miter box or table saw
12	¾" x ¼" plastic molding, 22-¼" long (on the long edge), ends cut at 45 degrees using a miter box or table saw
3	¼" hardware cloth, cut to leave no sharp edges, 22" x 22"
1	porcelain lamp socket
1	800 watt ceramic bulb heating element
1	120 v. thermostat with probe
1	120 v. muffin fan
1	Junction box with cover
1	Switch box
1	Strain relief for switch box
1	Light switch
1	25", 16 gauge extension cord
2	2" x 2" piece of reflective insulation
2	1" x 2" piece of reflective insulation
150	¾" wood screws
20	1" wood screws or deck screws
30	⁵⁄₁₆" staples
4	¼" lag bolts, self tapping on one end, and threaded ¼-20 on the other.
4	Large ¼" hole flat washers
4	¼"-20 wing nuts

Plywood

This project requires six 2" x 2" pieces of ⅜" finished plywood. I bought them precut. When you do this, the actual dimensions are

23-¾" x 23-¾". This is what accounts for the odd lengths of some of the lumber. If you buy larger pieces and cut it yourself, you'll end up with the same size due to the amount of material removed by the saw. If your pieces are slightly larger, you can either cut them to 23-¾" or change the dimensions of the other wood pieces to compensate.

Lay out your six pieces of plywood, and label each one of them with its intended location. Save the best piece (the one with the least warping) for the door.

Lumber

Cut your lumber to the specified dimensions. The 1" x 2" lumber is used for internal bracing, as well as the single piece of 1" x 3" lumber. The two pieces of 1-½" x 1-½" lumber are skids for holding the dehydrator off the floor. You can substitute 2" x 3" lumber or anything else you have handy.

Cut the 1" x 2" lumber into four pieces, each 23-¾" long. Label these pieces "A." Then cut three pieces, each 22-¼" long, label them as "C." Cut four more pieces of 1" x 2" lumber 19-⅞" long, and label them as "B." Finally, cut a piece of 1" x 3" lumber 22-¼" long, labeling it as "D."

The pieces for the skids underneath the dehydrator can be any dimensional lumber at least one inch in one dimension. Cut them 18" long and label as "E."

Insulation

The reflective insulation usually comes in rolls, so you'll end up with more than you need, but any you have left over can be used in an attic or chicken coop.

Cut four pieces of reflective insulation, two pieces will be 8" x 22", one piece will be 21" x 21" and the remaining piece will be 22" x 22".

After these are cut, cut an 6" diameter hole centered at 11-¼" x 8" of the largest piece of insulation. This cutout is for the porcelain

light receptacle at the bottom of the box. Label your insulation. The small pieces are labeled as "side," the largest is labeled "bottom," and the remaining piece is labeled "door."

Sides

Mark opposite ends of each side with a line ⅜" from the edge. Align board A lengthwise along the line, with the ends flush with the edges of the side. Attach using five #6 ¾" wood screws, and then repeat on the opposite end using board A. Attach the B boards even with the edge of each side so that the ends contact the A boards, and attach with five #6 ¾" wood screws. The edges with board A set back ⅜" are the top and bottom of the sides.

Bottom and Back

Attach the back to the sides by using five #6 ¾" wood screws drilled through the back into one of the B boards on each side. Then affix the bottom by drilling wood screws through the bottom into one of the A boards on each side. Attach the bottom to the back by using board C and drilling wood screws through the back and bottom respectively into board C.

Skids

Attach the skids to the bottom using 1-½" wood screws drilled from the inside of the bottom into the skids. The skids should be evenly spaced front to back and 1" in from the sides.

Mark for Muffin Fan

It's unlikely you'll get the same muffin fan I did. I got mine from All Electronics (model CF-120) for $15. Mark the center of the back

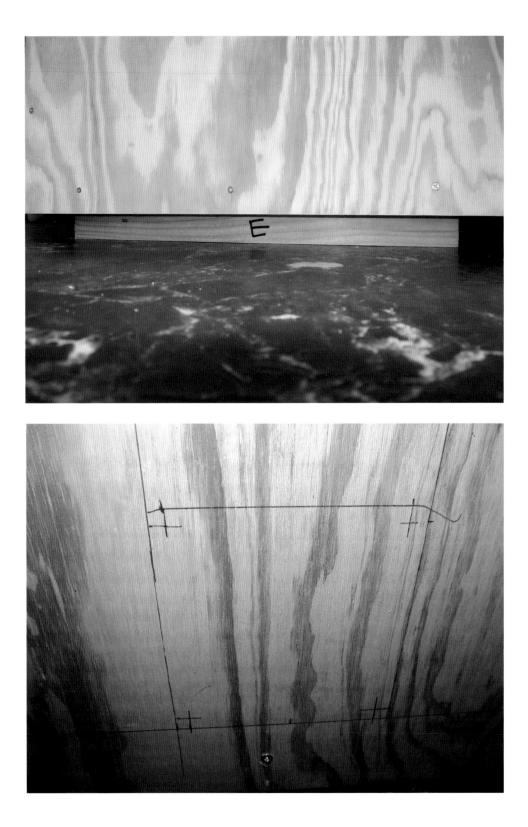

just above board C, then place your muffin fan level, draw around it, and mark where the holes for the bolts go.

Drill ³⁄₁₆" holes for the mounting bolts for the fan, and then use a reciprocating saw to cut out a hole for the air to blow through.

Install Light Fixture

Use a 3" hole saw to put a hole in the bottom of the dehydrator. Mark the center of the hole at 11-¼" from the inside edge of board A, and 8" from the inside edge of board C.

Now cut a 40" section of extension cord, and use it to wire the porcelain light fixture. Note: hot goes to the brass screw, neutral goes to the silver screw, and ground goes to the green screw. By convention, the black wire is hot, the white is neutral, and the green is ground. (See my note in the Wire the Electrical section on asking a friend for help if need be.)

Pass the piece of extension cord through the hole out the bottom of the dehydrator, and secure the light fixture using 1" wood screws.

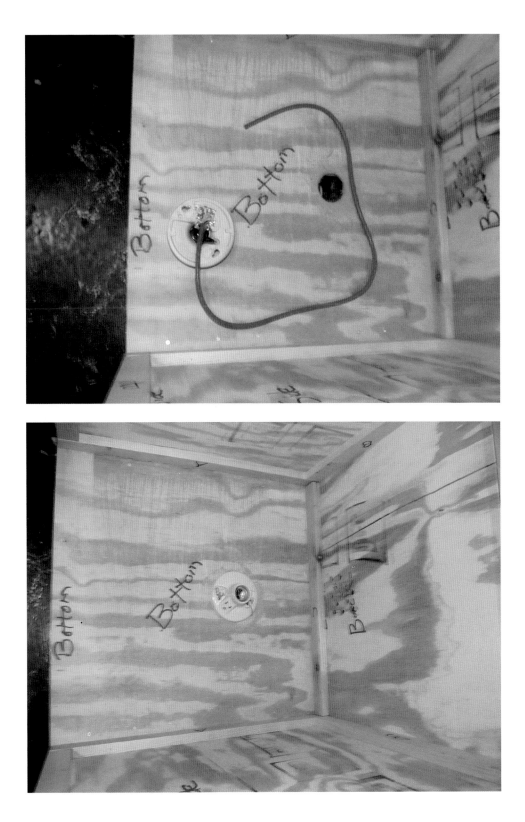

Install Rails

The parts list specifies using ¾" quarter round plastic molding for the rails, but many other things could also be used. For my dehydrator, I used metal shelving brackets cut to the correct length. The distance between rails is determined by the height of the racks, because the rack needs enough room to slide in between the rails upon which it rests and the rails immediately above. The distance between the bottom of the top rail and the top of the lower rail should be the height of the rack plus ¼".

I specify this because there are a lot of different ways you can frame the racks, some of which require more height than others. In the materials list, I specified 1-½" high plastic molding on top, and ¼" plastic molding on the bottom. Taking into account the height of the wire wedged between the pieces of molding, the height of the rack is about 2", so you'd need 2-¼" between the bottom of the top rail and the top of the next rail down. You can use ¾" quarter

round plastic molding instead of the 1-½" molding, thereby allowing the racks to be closer together and more racks to fit in the machine if you'd like. It would also be cheaper!

If you are using the parts specified in the materials list, mark each of the B uprights, measured from the bottom, at 18", 15-¾", 13-½", and 11-¼". These marks align with the top of each set of rails. Install the rails using wood screws drilled into the B uprights.

Wire the Electrical

If you don't know the difference between hot, neutral, and ground—find a friend who can help you before undertaking this. House current is serious business and doing this wrong can kill you, burn down your house, or at best blow a breaker.

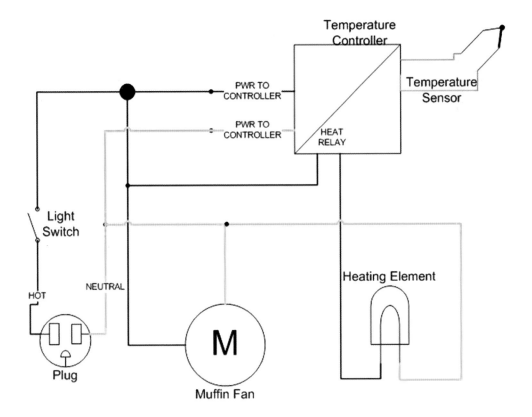

The objective of the wiring is straightforward: power is routed from an eight foot piece of extension cord (containing the male plug) through a light switch. When the switch is on, the fan is always on, but the power to the ceramic heater is controlled by the thermostat. The thermostat has a sensor that is placed in the upper front of the unit, just above the top rack.

The wiring will differ if you use a different thermostat unit. The one I am using is an Elitech STC-1000 that I ordered from Amazon. This particular device cost $17 and reads in Celsius degrees. The following diagram is for this particular unit, but others will work similarly. The accompanying illustrations give practical detail to how the diagram is implemented:

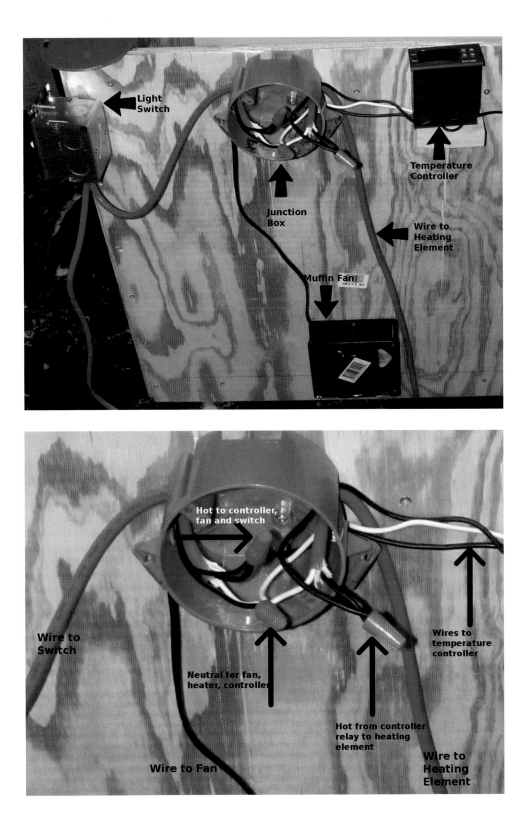

The Top

The top is now affixed on top of the A boards on the sides and the D board in the back. Drill through the top board into the A boards and D board using 1" wood screws. Then, use a drill and a ⅜" bit to drill 20–25 holes throughout the top as illustrated. These serve to allow moisture to escape under pressure from the fan.

The Door

There are many ways to attach doors to boxes. In this case, because I want I decent seal without having to use weather stripping, I have decided to avoid hinges.

Draw lines parallel to the top and bottom of the door, ½" in from the edge. Draw a second set of lines parallel to the sides of the

door, ¾" in from the edge. These serve as a guide for positioning the final two boards.

Attach the two remaining C boards so that their narrow edge contacts the plywood of the door. They should run in alignment lengthwise along the marks parallel to the top and bottom of the door, and their ends should align with the marks parallel to the sides of the door.

This door is attached using four ¼" lag bolts, one end being self-tapping and the other end using a standard ¼" 20 thread-per-inch threading.

Put the door onto the dehydrator, and drill four ¼" holes through the door into the B uprights. The top holes are centered 4" from the top and ⅜" from the edge. The bottom holes are centered 4" from the bottom and ⅜" from the edge. If necessary, use a level with your drill because you want these holes to be as close to perfectly straight as possible.

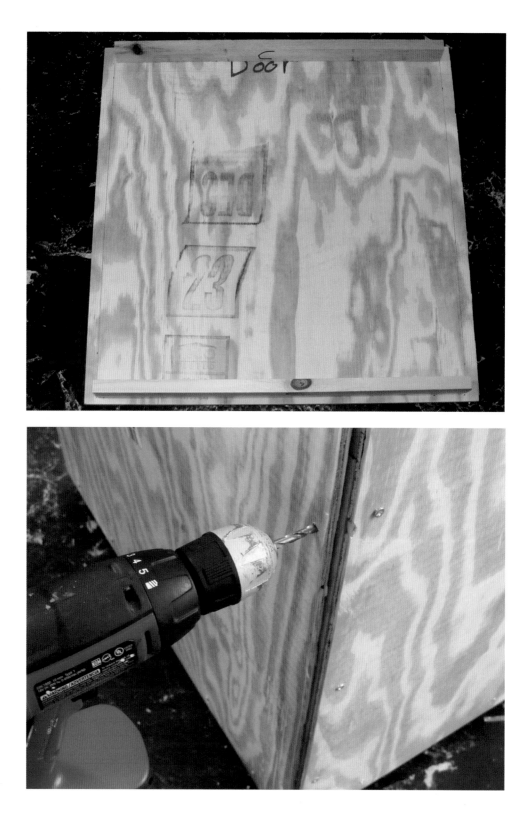

Take off the door, and drill the holes in the door only (not in the uprights) out to ⅜". Then install the lag bolts. The lag bolts can be easily installed by threading ¼"-20 nuts all the way down, and then using a deep socket or a box-end ⁷⁄₁₆" wrench to screw them in. Remove the nuts, and then put the door in place on the dehydrator,

with the lag bolts protruding through the holes in the door. Then put a large flat washer over each lag bolt, and secure the door with wing nuts.

Install the Insulation

Remove the door and use a staple gun and $\frac{5}{16}$" staples to attach the 21" x 21" piece of reflective insulation to the inside of the door. Center the insulation top to bottom and side to side. Then use $\frac{5}{16}$" staples to install the 22" x 22" piece of reflective insulation on the bottom, being sure to center the hole around the light fixture so the insulation isn't touching the light fixture. Finally, use the staples to install the two 8" x 22" pieces of insulation along the sides, beneath the bottom rail.

Make the Racks

As described earlier, the racks are made from ¼" mesh hardware cloth sandwiched between two pieces of plastic molding. This is both inexpensive and washable. See the earlier section on installing the rails regarding the effect the choice of molding will have on the spacing of the rails.

Mainly so it will show up better in pictures, I have used 1-½" x ¾" plastic molding for the top, and ¼" x ¾" plastic molding on the bottom. Each piece is cut with a 45 degree miter similar to the molding around door frames, with the long edge of each piece precisely 22-¼" long. You should always use the ¼" x ¾" flat molding on the bottom, but as long as the molding is ¾" wide, you can choose another height of molding for the top—even another piece of the same molding used for the bottom.

Cut your hardware cloth to 21-¾" x 21-¾". Then, use ¾" wood screws to secure the top and bottom pieces with the hardware cloth sandwiched between them. Then, if you are using taller molding like that illustrated, secure the junctions in the top molding using ¾" wood screws as well.

Check to make sure it fits the dehydrator, then make the rest of your racks.

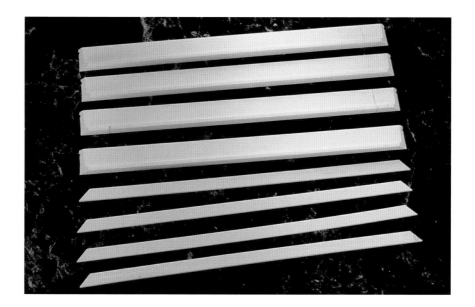

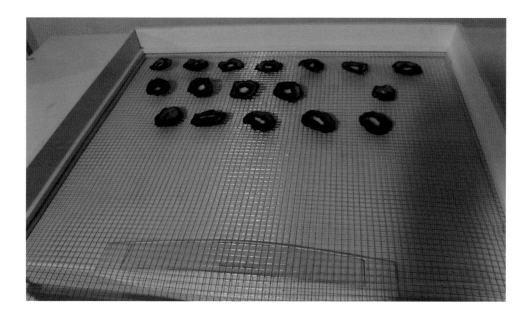

Test it Out!

You can use practically anything to test it out, but I chose kiwi as I had a few sitting around that I feared would go bad before I ate them. Here they are before the test: And here they are after:

Fahrenheit to Celsius Conversion

Throughout this book I have given dehydrating temperatures in Fahrenheit degrees. But a lot of the less expensive temperature controllers operate in Celsius degrees. The follow conversion chart should be helpful.

Fahrenheit	Celsius	Fahrenheit	Celsius
100	37.8	145	62.8
110	43.3	150	65.6
120	48.9	155	68.3
130	54.4	160	71.1
135	57.2	165	73.9
140	60	170	76.7

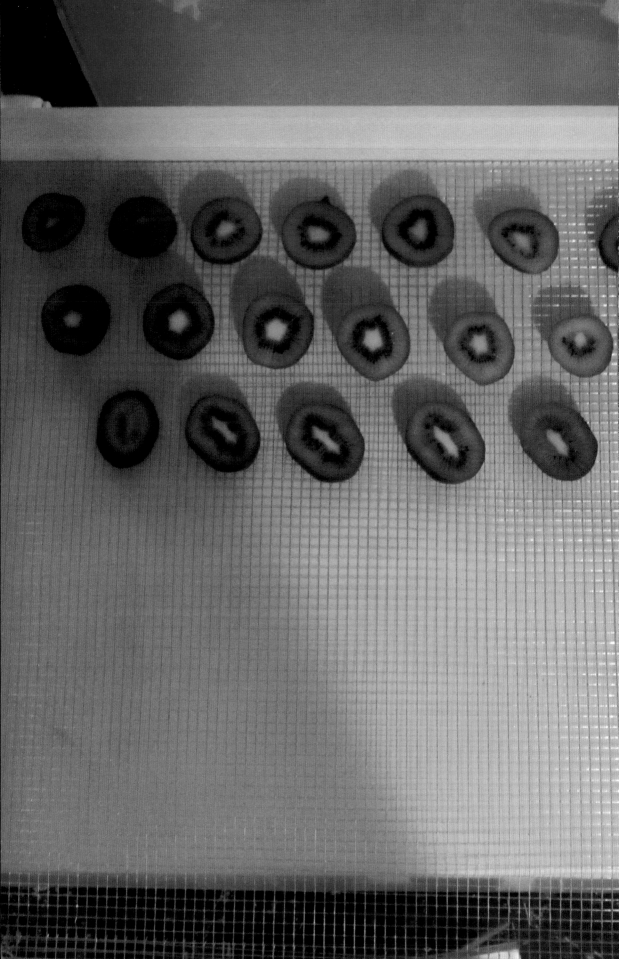

Notes

Recipe Journal

COOKING

US $14.95/CAN $19.95

BESTSELLING AUTHOR of the Mini Farming series, self-sufficiency expert Brett Markham turns his attention to the timeless art of food dehydrating.

An avid food dryer for years, Brett walks you through the simple steps for dehydrating everything from traditional classics like apples and jerky to more unusual fare. Whether you're following a raw food lifestyle or looking for new ways to make the most of your garden produce, this is an inside look at all aspects of dehydrating.

The Food Dehydrating Bible includes:

- **Straightforward instructions**
- **The science and history behind food dehydration**
- **Easy-to-follow recipes**
- **Diagrams**
- **Color photographs**
- **And more!**

This is a must-have manual for beginners and dehydrating gurus alike!

BRETT L. MARKHAM is an engineer, third-generation farmer, and polymath. Using the methods explained in his book, he runs a profitable, Certified Naturally Grown mini farm on less than half an acre. Brett works full-time as an engineer for a broadband ISP and farms in his spare time. He lives in New Ipswich, New Hampshire.

Skyhorse Publishing, Inc.
New York, New York
www.skyhorsepublishing.com

ISBN-10: 1-62914-181-X
ISBN-13: 978-1-62914-181-7

9 781629 141817

51495

Cover design by Kisscut Design
Printed in China